The aim of the *Earth Quest* series is to examine and explain how shamanic principles can be applied in the journey towards self-discovery – and beyond.

Each person's Earth quest is the search for meaning and purpose in their life – it is the establishment of identity and the realization of inner potentials and individual responsibility.

Each book in the series examines aspects of a life science that is in harmony with the Earth and shows how each person can attune themselves to nature. Each book imparts knowledge of the Craft of Life.

Beautiful Painted Arrow

Joseph E. Rael, whose Indian name is Beautiful Painted Arrow, is an internationally respected visionary, shaman and master storyteller of the Ute and Pueblo Indian traditions. He has spent many years giving lectures and workshops around the world, and has set up specially designed sound chambers in which people chant for world peace. He has also spoken to an Assembly at the United Nations on world peace. This is the first time that the teachings of this remarkable man have been made available to the general reader.

Beautiful Painted Arrow

STORIES AND TEACHINGS FROM THE NATIVE AMERICAN TRADITION

Joseph E. Rael
(Beautiful Painted Arrow)

ELEMENT
Shaftesbury, Dorset ● Rockport, Massachusetts

© Joseph E. Rael 1992

Published in Great Britain in 1992 by
Element Books Limited
Longmead, Shaftesbury, Dorset

Published in the USA in 1992 by
Element, Inc
42 Broadway, Rockport, MA 01966

Illustration by Martin Rieser
Cover design by Max Fairbrother
Typeset by Poole Typesetting (Wessex) Ltd
Printed and bound in Great Britain by
Dotesios Ltd, Trowbridge, Wilts

A catalogue record for this book
is available from the British Library

Library of Congress data available

ISBN 1–85230–310–7

To Joe Scott, who continues to support the work and who has supported it since the very beginning.

Joseph Rael does us an important service in this unusual book: he gives us the opportunity to think and experience through an ancient language whose connection with Earth and Spirit are much more profound than English. *Beautiful Painted Arrow* helps us understand through the blending of two languages, two separate realities, that we each come as a gift to life: we are gemstones of awareness who, with conscious polishing, can be come more and more precious to the Great Circle of Life. Joseph helps us, with the wisdom of his native pueblo peoples approach, to polish the gem of our insightful/visionary life – our possibilities of full human awareness. His use of sound in the practices he offers is very illuminating and special – make good use of them!

Brooke Medicine Eagle
American native Earthkeeper, healer, teacher, creator of Eagle Song wilderness camps and author of *Buffalo Woman Comes Singing*.

Verbal or non-verbal language was created so that we could revert to 'original awareness'; words remind us that we are already enlightened, and that the language contains the keys that can open us up to the true potential in our lives.

As children, we hear sound associations in children's stories. When we grow up, our early memories put these sounds alongside our adult experiences, thereby bringing our daily experiences within the moral codes of early childhood teaching.

A circular image is used for the illustrations in this book because every moment is a circle of light which is for that moment the shield of personal experience in relationship to the metaphoric mind.

Contents

Acknowledgements

To my three sons and two daughters: Joseph Jr, who inspired me to write this book; George Steven, who danced this book for me in the Sun Dance of a few years ago; my youngest son, Mario, who encouraged me to play and rest while I was developing the ideas in *Beautiful Painted Arrow*; Geraldine for her support and patience, and Theresa for her belief in me.

To Marci Fabrici, who helped me put the final draft together.

And especially to my beloved friends Norma Kaplis and Jim Galvin and their Heart to Heart Foundation.

Introduction

THIS IS A BOOK ABOUT IDEAS, ideas expressed as metaphors alongside experiences because, like the leaves of a tree, they are the life source of the planetary culture. The leaves capture the light of the sun and feed the essence of the sun's rays through the branches to the trunk, then by way of the roots to the Mother Earth. In return the Mother returns the gifts to the whole tree as life sustenance.

The sun, the Father, in metaphor is the Mother's helper. Together they are the Spirit of Greatness. We, too, are constructed like the tree; we are made out of many ideas, like the leaves on a tree, and in time they produce their fruit. And in that way we give back to the Earth, which in return provides us with many more stories to live by, because ideas as metaphors alongside experience are the fruits of our search for essence.

From the time I was a child I had psychic abilities. When, at the age of seven I came to live with my father's Indian tribe, I was already becoming a natural visionary and had capacities to see beyond ordinary reality.

This book is as much about my visionary abilities as that of *metaphor alongside of experience*. And how you too can develop your visionary capacities through the process of the use of metaphor because you are God's gift to life. Therefore you are your own greatest example of God's living truth.

When I started to learn the Tiwa language spoken by my father's people, the Picuris Pueblo tribe of north central New Mexico, their spoken language saw everything in metaphors. Because I was also learning to speak English at that time I began to make word use comparisons between the Tiwa and English words. My mother would say, 'Go bring the dog' in English, and in Tiwa my comparison to what she was saying became: 'Bring the being who watches over us.' Or she might say something simple like 'Sit down' in English, and in Tiwa that would mean 'Allow greatness to alight there'. 'Wipe the table' became for me 'Clean the face of Goodness'. Even the name Beautiful Painted Arrow that I carry to this day is a metaphor: Beautiful (*koye*) means 'the Beautiful One'; Painted (*tah*) means 'sacred symbols on the arrow shaft'; and Arrow (*slew*) means 'that which has warmth'.

Every winter, as was our tradition, the Picuris children's stories were told in metaphor. I began to bridge the two worlds, the literal words of English to the metaphors in the Tiwa language. It was at this time that I began to search for metaphors in the English language too, and in most cases they were quite imaginative. 'Go bring the dog' could mean bringing the dog in a large bucket to my mother, or carrying our large collie over my left shoulder, or in my arms.

Metaphor is 'Awareness that is Awake', the experience is that which is occurring from that place in us that is *Believing We Exist* and the different parts of our physical bodies connect us to insights.

Once again this book is about metaphor and experience, and how the Picuris children's stories, as metaphors, could become actual natural visionary experiences later on in my ordinary adult life.

Reading between the Gaps

WE ENTER A DREAM STATE WHEN experiencing visionary insight, in that everything moves in slow motion. This is not to say that this is what actually happens, but it certainly feels that way for me. A part of us goes into a place of 'detached participation', in that our attention span becomes totally merged in the moment and in the metaphoric experience. This detached sense of what is unfolding allows us to enjoy the experience without any sense of impending danger. In other words, we feel safe.

In the moment of the visionary state there also seems to exist a quiet splendour. Another way of describing this condition is that 'awareness is over-riding the controlling self', or that part of us that sees in polarities, that is, good or bad, and that wants to be in charge. It gives up all its rights to control the moment, and the mind reconciles the vision or insight, so that one feels no separation between the personal and universal self.

The insight for me was that when we are in control of our actions, words or deeds, we are 'soul talking' as in verifying our existence, or, in other words 'Believing We Exist'. In those moments within a visionary experience we become the metaphor of 'Awareness that is Awake', and in this state the mind does not care whether it truly exists but simply merges with and becomes the 'transmission of what is', or the passing of a message, as in insight.

In the Picuris children's story of Magpietail Boy (see page 57), the Wizards try to bridge the gaps between opposite walls by building rainbows of light with parts of their bodies. Now here I would like to say that in the name 'Magpietail Boy' is that part of us that 'Believes We Exist'. The name of Magpietail Boy too embodies the understanding that that which we believe in is only one of the parts of true reality, or thinking, and if we use it by itself it will lead us further away from truth. But when we use this understanding with awakened awareness we are living out of insight. The story teller reveals that the Wizards took Magpietail Boy down the stepladder, and sat him by Yellow Corn Woman. One insight is that prior to the moment when one becomes the experience of the visionary state, 'Believes We Exist' is carried down into inner 'Awakened Awareness'. Thus the two worlds of belief and awareness are joined, and new insight can be gleaned.

The story relates that Magpietail Boy fell asleep on the lap of Yellow Corn Woman. This means that during the bridging of the gaps the be-ing of 'Believes We Exist' must go to sleep, for 'Awakened Awareness' is the door that opens and allows the bridging of the gaps. Another insight is that the walls that the Wizards are attempting to bridge in the Magpietail Boy myth are the unclarities of the personal self versus those of the universal self.

The story continues that he is put on a cliff bench and left there. This metaphor means to me that a jump in realization has occurred, because now the story teller takes us back out of the inner universal self to the outer physical landscape. Here again we must revert to the outer struggle experiences of the be-ing of 'Believing We Exist'.

And how do we achieve the opening of this door? Well, the story, 'The Journey with the Mermen' (page 49), where I am taken down onto the ocean floor by the three Mermen, symbolized for me that there are three constituent parts of the play in this visionary experience. In hindsight my conclusions are that first, the physical salt content of my body was normal, neither too high nor too low; second, the sugar content in my physical body was also at a normal level, and the third step was the falling down into the ocean of Awakened Awareness, where insight was given to me by a cosmic King-like image in meta-phor. He instructed me to build a fire which means 'to make a connec-tion between the world of Believing We Exist and the world of 'Aware-ness that is Awake', and this was the place of new insight or of a visionary experience. It seems that fasting, and exercising in order to sweat the body fluids, can be an important way to induce the visionary state. Also, intentional suffering as in marathon dancing, helps to break down the blockages placed there by the ego for the protection and security of the physical being of the being of 'Believes We Exist'.

But there is still more here as to why movement works. Briefly put, I am involved in activity in all of the visionary experiences in the stories in this book. In 'Sandy, the Runaway Horse' (page 9), for instance, there is the action or motion of running. In 'My Grandfather' (page 13) there is singing and dancing, and the action of walking into a wall into a vision. In 'The Mountain Race' (page 17), there is running, and the shift to alternative states of reality. 'Appearing and Disappearing' (page 25) and 'In the Springtime' (page 21) talk about the moment in which the activity of 'Believing We Exist' merges with and strengthens 'Awareness that is Awake'. However, this example does not fully explain to us the *why* of activity, as in how or why work activity brings or stimulates insight or new vision.

The chapter entitled 'Insights' explains the how or why of the human condition, in life works, of how insights occur when we slip and fall into a hole beyond our understanding made in the solid ground of our 'Believing We Exist'.

In the chapters 'St Stephen's Church of the Sacred: The Angel in the Cave' (page 29), 'The Pumas' (page 33), 'At the Waterfall' (page 41), 'The Journey with the Mermen' (page 49) and the children's stories of Magpietail Boy (page 57), Sengerepove'ena and his fight with the Sun (page 69), the Old Giantess and the brother and sister fawns (page 75) the quality of metaphors and experience is examined.

In 'The Six Passions' I attempt to show how these can be put to positive insightful living. All of the insights that make up the test are found at the end of the book, and learning how to think through the use of the five vowel sounds explains how to use the English language to see the metaphor within it, and, in the 'How and Why Insight Occurs', shows how insight happens. In the last chapter I review and bring forth in the summation the full meaning of the individual chapters.

The first part of the book is written interchangeably between Tiwa thought and English, and so I have italicized all of the Tiwa metaphors.

I have numbered the insights in the book to help the flow of ideas, and because I wanted to list them at the end of the book for the convenience of the reader. This is not to say that the insights listed are the only ones I received but rather that you, the reader, will have an opportunity to glean your own insights. And finally, after each story, I have created a practice for those who are ready to meet the being of Awakened Awareness, or simply to enjoy.

PART ONE

1 Sandy, the Runaway Horse

SANDY WAS THE NAME OF A BLACK HORSE my father had just broken to work in a team. On Sandy's first work day my father hitched him to the mower, as we were going to cut alfalfa fields on the other side of the river. I rode with my father while he held the reins and guided the horses across the river. Sandy pranced handsomely, and although he acted wildly at one point, remained fairly calm. But when we got to the fields the cutting noises frightened him so my father sat me up on Sandy's shoulders and I rode him, because he was more accustomed to the saddle than he was to a mower. I remember his awesome power beneath me, his snorting and the smell of the freshly cut alfalfa.

On our way home my father dropped the reins, got down and opened the wire gate. As he was returning to the horses the team began to canter away, with me sitting helplessly on Sandy's back. As the horses gained speed, I saw pictures in my mind, coming from my father. One of them was of *me falling into the river, and the other was of me letting myself drop on to a clump of willows*. Not realizing that my father was communicating telepathically, hoping that I would *fall in the river* or *on the willows*, I chose to hold on for dear life. As the horses galloped faster and faster, I clung even more tightly to the two forks on the harness collars. The up-and-down motion of the horses sent hot and cold chills through me, and with the continued jerking motions my head hit one of the square iron tops, and it broke my skull. During my teenage years I realized that during times of rapidly changing events, or emotions, such as fear moving on to panic, my mental telepathic capabilities were increased enormously.

Next I remembered many exploding, flying stars and then an all-enveloping quiet, darkness. I do not recall anything after that until I woke up at the Taylor Hospital in the presence of a nurse. I checked my head; it was covered with bandages and hurt when these were removed daily by the doctor. There seemed to be a hotness and coldness in the pain. It was during this time that I watched *the top of my head through the doctor's eyes, and sometimes through those of the nurses as well.* The unexpected sensation of the hot and cold levels pulsing in my body when the doctor removed the bandages helped me to see what he was doing.

For the reader, INSIGHT 1: I want to share in 'Crossing the River', listening with my ears and seeing with my eyes so that my whole body was listening, because 60 per cent of what I was hearing was being received by my physical body, and 40 per cent was being received by my eyes. I used mental telepathy when I saw my falling experience in my father's thoughts. In 'Sandy, the Runaway Horse' feeling the hot and cold chills seemed to help heighten my telepathic capacities.

It was at this point in my life that I began to associate the physical to action to insight, but it was not until my later years that I could see my physical body's other connections with insight.

Practice

Step 1   Sit quietly in a room, and visualize a framed picture opposite you, showing a beautiful meadow with a clump of willows in the distance, and just beyond that, a river. Visualize a beautiful black horse named Sandy, and see yourself sitting on his back for a moment. Gently tap his sides with your heels until you feel his back begin to move. Feel the power of Sandy's vibration.

Step 2   As you ride through the meadow, imagine you are approaching the willow trees. Remember that the willow is a water-succulent plant, and see the reflected light from the river vibrating through the trees.

Step 3   Bring Sandy to a standstill next to the willows. *Imagine* yourself, in slow motion, falling off Sandy's back into the clump of light-filled red willows. Let their light bring you into enlightenment.

Step 4   Lie in the willows until you feel your body filled with light.

Step 5   Next, get back on to Sandy's back and ride over to the edge of

the river. Imagine yourself once again falling slowly into the water to release any grief or sadness. This will be highly beneficial because this is the 'River of Forgetfulness': its water symbolizes light, and has the capacity to wash away as well as to create a form.

Step 6   Visualize yourself emerging from the river free of grief and sadness and still radiating with light. Climb back upon Sandy's back and ride back the way you came.

Step 7   Re-enter your body as once again you see the picture frame, and the image of a beautiful meadow.

Reminder to the reader: in these stories, all the Tiwa metaphors and my Grandfather's words are italicized.

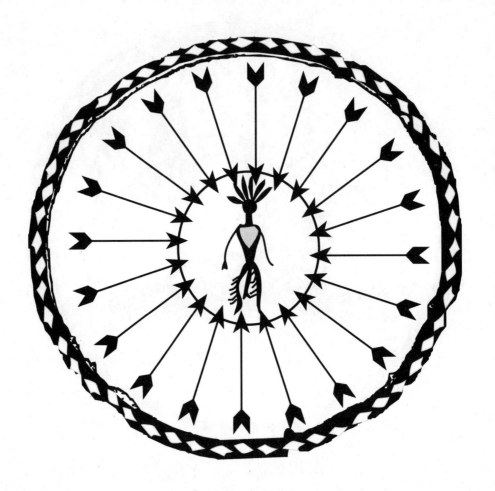

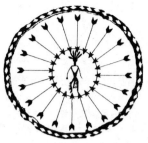

2 My Grandfather

WHEN MY GRANDFATHER WAS NOT RIDING in his horse-drawn wagon, he could be seen running everywhere. He was always running between his winter village home and his summer ranch, to the south-west. His long braids would sometimes get caught in the wind and fly around, so he used to tie them round his neck. He used to say that they represented the line that separates the sky from the earth of the physical body. When my grandfather tied a cloth around his neck, it was *to keep vigilance so that the thinking of the heart remained connected*. Whenever he did this for himself, he was actually doing it on behalf of all the people.

He used to take the soles off his 'store-bought' shoes, as we used to call them, and replace them with the skins of deer, elk or sometimes cowhide. He used to say, '*We are walking stories: the more we walk, the more stories reveal themselves. Our shoe soles help us to see. Deer vision is one; elk vision is another, and cow still another. Animals connect us to our guides.*'

My grandfather was of the curing society so the people used to come to him for help. A Pueblo myth of creation says that 'They moved on, but they still had headache and stomachache. They still needed something. They knew they needed doctors. Four doctors were made. These were members of curing societies; they gave the people medicine.'[1] This is the migration story of the people moving from the underworld to the upper world. One day, when I was playing really hard, my left knee became dislocated, and my grandfather massaged it back into place. He used black ashes to heat it up before he pulled it back into position, and immediately afterwards I felt a coldness throughout my body. When there was strife in the community, or differences or difficulties between family members, he used to counsel, '*The people who are most against you are the ones that need you the most. So forgive them and then give them your help.*'

When I was a child at Picuris Pueblo, he used to take me with him to pray the Christian rosary for wakes in the nearby villages of Vadito, Penasco, Rio`Lucio or Chamisal. Our friendship grew, and in time he wanted me near when he rehearsed his chants or practised ancient ceremonies. I became his 'go-getter' or apprentice, so I felt very privi-leged. He was firm and direct when necessary, but at other times he was gentle and kind.

One night he invited me to sleep in his ceremonial chamber. When I awoke in the morning the whole room was translucent and everything was resonating with sound. A beautiful chorus was coming from the ceremonial paraphernalia. Yellow, red and white lines that he had drawn on the ceremonial floor were lifting up and down inside beautiful musical sounds. I looked to where he was standing by the stepladder at the kiva entrance, the opening to his underground ceremonial chamber. He caught my stare and asked with concern, 'What is wrong with you?' And I answered immediately, *'Your body and the whole room are singing.'* I watched his facial expression change from deep thought to delight, and for a few seconds even his laughter had a special beautiful resonating quality.

He never explained what happened. All he said was that *everything is alive and singing its own song and that we, the two-leggeds, are our own chants. He was asking me to be present and in each moment.* Tiwa has multiple meanings to each word and will have other spiritual or philoso-phical meanings besides the ones used here.

One day I saw him walk into a place beyond the walls of the chamber, and when I asked him about that he answered by saying that *not everything that we see or believe may be as real as we may think it is.*

'Nowia,' he said, *'is night time, when we sleep in order to seek what we cannot find when we are awake.'* He always talked in riddles, so I used great concentrative powers of focus in an attempt to understand his answers, frequently to no avail. Later in my life I realized that he alternated between 'Believing We Exist' and 'Awakened Awareness'.

One day he asked me to focus on the opposite wall, and to watch for any signs of movement. *Focus is designed to penetrate beyond the veils of aware consciousness because ordinary reality is made up of overlay upon overlay of alternate realities.* I began to stare, and as he sang and drummed a strange light sparked alive on the dark, earthen wall and began to grow larger and larger. *Singing places of 'the people' or of the human body can bring us revelations.* It was like looking into a cinema screen, and the daylight emanating from it lit up the room. At one point he asked me to watch for a person or an animal, and he repeatedly emphasized that I must not take my eyes away from the vision. He then said, *'I am going into it and I want you to watch me and keep looking until I come back into the room. Be sure now. Keep watching and do not look away.'*

I saw his physical body walk straight into the light and on until he disappeared over the horizon. After a while he returned with something in his hands, and as he crossed back into the chamber where I had been waiting, the screen became smaller and smaller until we were in a dark room once again. All I can remember is that I felt as if my body had been washed with light, and was totally pure. On the floor next to a sacred painted form were the flowers and herbs from an alternative summer-time reality; yet for us it was winter at the Picuris Pueblo in 1943.

I still think of him as he was walking in the vision, moving away from me in his buckskin leggings and beaded moccasins, his red blanket up to his waist, walking slowly to a place beyond our chamber walls. The sky was dark blue and the trees were casting small shadows because it was mid-day, and there was a soft breeze blowing waves of grasses north to south. The lights of the day were bright all around. He became my hero; he could perform the kind of magic that demonstrated that we can live in alternating realities where the unexpected, the miracle or the afterthought are more the rule than the exception.

I wonder sometimes today whether, if I had closed my eyes, he would have disappeared from the vision. 'Do you think I can walk through walls too?' I asked a day later and he answered, *'You should try to do something different because I have already done this.'*

During my teenage years at Picuris, I sometimes wondered if life was real or a dream, because there was always something unusual going on. When I was with him I came to expect the unexpected, for the play of lights around him was always changing.

In summary, the question 'Do you think I can walk through walls too?' essentially asks if I could physically do what he did. What my grandfather was suggesting was that when one human being makes a breakthrough in consciousness (as he had done in walking through walls) no one would have to repeat this action. Anyone is capable of doing it at anytime he or she wants, because the initial step has already been taken by another human being.

INSIGHT 2: Whatever we see or experience outside our physical body (or what I call our 'outer landscape') teaches our inner landscape, thereby imparting meaning by way of the physical body. To have insight is when the whole body hears and acts upon what it is experiencing, beyond the pre-condition of Believing We Exist, so that the awareness of metaphor can bring fresh knowledge as insight.

Practice

Step 1   Sit quietly on a chair. After taking six long breaths, imagine that you are sitting inside a bubble of light.

Step 2   Imagine that because you are inside this bubble you are protected, and that you can travel into other universes, the archetypes that make up the different levels of consciousness located within your physical body.

Step 3   Tell yourself that you want to travel in this bubble into your right foot. Not because you want to see any injury, but because you want to see that particular aspect of the macrocosm within your microcosm, and how the macrocosm resonates within you.

This practice can be expanded, and used to explore different parts of ourselves, the microcosm, and as a result, we can see different perspectives of the macrocosm. This is an essentially stimulating practice because by exploring the microcosm of the body, you can discover the higher realms of consciousness that pertain to the macrocosm.

3   The Mountain Race

IN THE BEGINNING, FIRST WAS THE DREAM (association) and then came the vision (observation).

Running is what the universal *law* is doing and *in that moment when we see someone running everything becomes placement and awareness.* In this example *the moment is like a person who understands like a normal human being and is perceiving what is happening.*

The mountain runners brought the dream-seeing force from the mountain spirits to the Picuris village people. *The heart is the mountain. It is the middle of the circle and the centre of life. The people of long ago had come to live inside the heart of the great mystery. In running we irrigate all those places in our bodies with the sweetness of our blood that comes from our hearts. For we are spirits of the sacred mountains.*

The sound of the runners of that springtime race filled the canyons. Chasing close behind me, following, shouting, asking that I run faster, was my grandfather. It was only for a moment that I saw him. The race was on. I tried to run my fastest, but he kept up with me, still shouting that I try even harder. After the first four miles I found a comfortable stride, and kept at that pace until we came into view of Picuris. He had fallen back, but then he increased his stride and was, again, upon me, shouting, 'A-ma-pai, path of the infinite (Hurry up! to the light of wisdom *that creates the place of no thought); of Awakened Awareness'.*

It happened silently, quickly, and came as a strong and renewing force of strength. It overcame me, so that I felt as if I had wings; and while I could hear my feet striking the earthen pathway, I was the Universal Self breathing. His shouts faded away until I could only vaguely hear them. The villagers' shouted sounds of encouragement became barely audible because a roaring sound grew louder within me,

burying their voices in my head, enlivening them still further. They also gave a reality to the spirit of the eagle that I had become as I entered into the village itself. My physical body was fading. It was appearing and disappearing. In those moments, in a flash of light, I saw the Earth in miniature, running and breathing, and understood that my physical body was made of *conscious associations* of the Earth, clay and sky breath.

INSIGHT 3: When the physical heart is pumping the physical blood of the body it is affirming the act; the blood is receptivity and the action of the physical body is reconciliation. The speed of my running was the purpose of the race, because speed is the metaphor for the lifting of consciousness up to the level of cosmic thought. Why? Because all physical worlds were made from speeding light. I was experiencing the shift that I choose to share with you in this practice.

Practice

Step 1   Imagine that you are sitting quietly in the middle of a circle, and begin to breath slowly but consciously. Visualize a waterfall washing and purifying you; see yourself standing simultaneously in all four corners of a square made out of light, and see the relationship between those four corners; see everything around you in wonderful clarity; see yourself as an infant, imagine that you are in a state of total innocence, yet lying on a bed made up of blankets of awesome power, and feel those cushiony blankets feeding your soul with resonance. Now see yourself being lifted up on two giant hands, and know that it is the Great Mystery that is raising you to places of higher and higher revelations that you will encounter after you have finished this exercise.

Step 2   Remember that this practice is important because it will strengthen the heart muscles, as does physical running.

4   In the Springtime

My uncle, Pedro Martinez, was a Picuris Pueblo elder who came to be one of my teachers. I used to visit him when we were not working together in the fields. I also spent a lot of time with him during the time of World War II, when we lived at the ranch at Poo-ohh-ma. We developed a deep mutual friendship.

'We live in our skins, unfolding the sacred knowledge only as new insights appear acceptable to use. Life never created anything outside of goodness,' he would say, 'so run the sacred.'

He would start watching me long before I knew he was there. One day I discovered he was playing with me, because he would stand where I could see him next to the ranch house, which was between our house and the mountain. I ran to and from the mountain every morning, and then suddenly he would have disappeared the next time I looked for him.

He was of the Kossa, a member of the clown society, and this Pueblo creation myth explains his society. 'The chiefs walked alone, they were very sorrowful. They said, "We need something", so they went back into Sand Lake. Then they brought some individuals called the Kossa, who are members of a clown society. They made fun, and at last the people began to laugh and grow glad again.'[2] The Indian clown is symbolic of the mental serum of the tribal society which in the human brain creates acceptance of the new, or the different, by the use of humour. In ancient times, as in today's society, the clown introduces new ideas or enlivens the old ones through humour. Additionally, the members of this society are considered as medicine people or healers. I think my uncle was teaching me to pay attention by appearing and disappearing unexpectedly.

I asked him once to teach me how to disappear and one day, pointing at the black fungus that was growing on an ear of corn, he said, *'Eat this black stuff and your stomach will get black so you can disappear.'* He was always telling jokes.

Pedro Martinez also taught me about feeding the Earth. He instructed, *'Run at dawn with the sacred corn meal, spilling it out of your right hand, and run that way feeding the holy places of our ancestry, the holy places of the people that give us life.'* Our dogs used to run with me up the mountain trails and our cats, ten of them, watched us from their high resting places. I used to run six miles before breakfast. I know the dogs came with me just for the fun of it and the cats, I was convinced, kept an account to make sure that we did. My foster father Agapito (Where Eagles Perch) used to say *you must always be ready to run in case we have a war and you have to run.* Father always made up different reasons for the various things we needed to do. One thing never changed though: the cats were always there watching, and the dogs were always running in the pre-dawn lights of our springs and summers.

Springtimes were full of early morning bird sounds, and strikingly beautiful sunrises of golden light filtering through the leaves of the aspen trees which surrounded our earthen water tank. We honored the aspen trees and water dam. *'The early morning running is our prayer to them, too.'* Agapito would say.

We used the water tank for storing the spring runoff, so we could irrigate the vegetable gardens and apricot trees. Ditch cleaning up the mountain was always fun, because I liked to see the rushing waterfalls as we climbed higher and higher into the mountains, and because we would take big picnic lunches. We sang songs to the many tributaries, too, connecting our water source to the dry lands of the lowland places where the crops waited for the life-giving moisture.

One day I wanted to play, and to do that I needed to run off with the dogs. Father was a great vibration reader of my mind. He said, *'Our sacred duty is to clean the veins that will bring the sweet waters of the mountain-heart to the fields of the Infinite Self. Otherwise, the plants will not grow and we will not have enough food to eat this winter. The village people are depending on us to do this work.'* His words inspired me because he talked so endearingly about the plants and the living spirits of the corn, alfalfa and wheat fields that even the tiniest thought about resting thereafter made me feel guilty. Most of the time he could convince me about my enthusiasm for work and at other times he would simply shout loudly, scaring me into what I now call work-appreciation.

And so it was, for we were, he and I, on a very sacred mission. So I put my heart and soul into the task of ditch cleaning and instilled into

myself a renewed determination. And although every once in a while I would catch a smile on his face, I thought perhaps he was only being happy.

My foster father Agapito Martinez, of the Picuris Pueblo, and my foster mother, Lucia Sandovel Martinez of the Jicarilla Apache of Dulee, New Mexico, raised me in their home after my mother passed away. They left the world of the living some years ago. However, I still think of my childhood with them.

INSIGHT 4: Hearing with my physical ears connected me directly to physical activity; I understood that work was another way of worshipping, that listening and working were one and the same thing. In running or working physical energy is exerted in a particular direction, towards a certain result, thereby generating an active energy of consciousness beyond our self-imposed limitations.

Practice

Step 1   Sit quietly in a chair, and in your imagination place a very large balloon over your house.

Step 2   Leave the balloon there, knowing that when you go to your job, do housework, jog, plant your garden, exercise, when you do anything that involves expending physical effort, the energy expended will go into the balloon.

Step 3   Understand that you may draw on this stored energy for your mental, emotional, physical or spiritual health whenever you need. It will always be there for you; you need only ask for it.

5 Appearing and Disappearing

I GREW UP IN THE MOUNTAINS as an only child, and in summer when the chores were done, I always found the energy to walk and run up to those behind our adobe house. In the early afternoons, in the ever-changing light on the pinon and pine forests, I would practise entering into the vast silence of our mountain, knowing that my task was to find the long shadows of late afternoon and the tracks of different animals. As the time passed the shadows would make the tracks invisible, and I would trail the mule deer with her fawns slowly and quietly long before I would see them. Sometimes they would spot me first, and so that meant I had lost the game of *'finding without being seen first'*.

Mostly I loved to walk, and to catch the long trails of migrating ants, to capture with my eyes birds nesting, birds with worms in their beaks flying towards their young ones, or counting the number of hops of the cottontail rabbits as they ran under bushes to hide. Why? Because the number of hops was connected to what might be happening cosmically. The game basically was to come up to the rabbits without scaring them or initiating their sharp, alert calls.

I used to practise the ceremony of singing to the different animal tracks, for *they were impressions of the animals*, and were *left as our gifts from the vast silence of the infinite*. And when I prayed and sang to them, the animals never ran, or were annoyed when I came upon them. Perhaps it was because of my early childhood teaching of *being seen rather than being heard*, and that my uncle had taught me well how to *disappear out of the consciousness of the moment*. The ancient warriors were trained in this way. Perhaps animals saw me in disbelief and stopped in curiosity. I always ran home from the mountain tops when it was well into dusk, when the trails were barely visible; but I had walked these paths so many times that I knew where every stone, tree or every turn

was down the mountainside. So often in those moments I felt I was more like the spirit of the trails following the path of the heart, and my physical body was along just for the fun of it.

As I grew older I carried my spirit into the realization that I could, and that it was all right, for me to carry my father's people.

INSIGHT 5: It is through culture that evolution occurs. The Tiwas believe that only through meritorious work and/or high ethical behaviour can one human being be awarded not only the highest potential but the opportunity of carrying the whole tribal essence in and of itself in the individual. And that once this responsibility is bestowed it is to be carried on the basis of continual vigilance, so that only the highest ethical behaviour be maintained.

In the mirror I saw in my face the many faces of people who had taught me and brought me up to live in the world of their dreamtime.

In chanting to the animal tracks the chanter brings 'The Maker of the Tracks' into the present tense, as into the here and now. For instance, by singing to the prints made by the animals a visual image is created in the thoughts of the singer, therefore acting as a plaster-of-Paris impression.

Practice

Step 1   Find an animal track and make a mould of it of a material that will harden, such as plaster-of-Paris, so that you will have a physical object to hold during this practice. You may use a print from your pet dog or cat.

Step 2   Sit in a chair and imagine that you are feeding the moulded print with a handful of sand particles – all sand is made of light crystals – and chant the vowel sounds of the animal's name. This process will connect you with the animal.

After living with the Tiwa language for a number of years, I began to speak and think in metaphors in English, because these lead to the inner primary intelligence, where words connected me to the inner meaning of ordinary language.

6　St Stephen's Church of the Sacred: The Angel in the Cave

IN JULY 1983 I RECEIVED A VISION. I saw that in the physical world we must go back to the oral tradition of all languages, and give spoken languages their rightful place next to the written word. The vision was saying that what we need in today's world is to re-acquaint ourselves with the vibrations emanating from the spoken word so that we might understand inner meaning. That mystical meaning can come through the physical body and the mind via sound.

The vision came when I had been sacred dancing, during which I had seen an androgynous being, which I was told was the cosmic mother/father principle. It transformed into an oval-shaped chamber, in which I saw men and women chanting. And so after the vision I travelled throughout the United States looking for a site to build the first sound chamber. Later that year I built one in Bernalillo, New Mexico, and after that I went to other places in the United States to present the idea of chambers and to locate sites for them. I also thought about taking the chambers to other countries since I already had one in Australia, and perhaps these plans provoked the half dream/half vision.

In the half dream/half vision that came to me in the early hours on a day in June, 1986, I was given specific instructions to fly to Austria for the purpose of constructing a sacred sound chamber high in the uplands near Graz. So it was that I made immediate plans to fly to Vienna, since I had already committed myself to building them all over the earth.

INSIGHT 6: When a vision or idea is received, the recipient also is given the power to carry it through because that is the nature of insight.

On the night we arrived in Vienna we stayed at a friend's house. It was 4am when an angel appeared at the foot of the bed, wearing a white gown with a white rope tied around his waist. He had long brown hair, was slender and about six feet tall. He communicated with me with his heart and said, 'Come with me. I have something to show you.'

In the next instant we were both gliding close to the ceiling down a corridor in a cave, that was very like two caves that I would soon see in physical reality. Below us were men, women and children wailing in great pain. As we reached the end of the tunnel we saw that the entrance was blocked, and the angel said to me, 'You are the one that can open the doorway and free them.'

To my surprise I shot a red beam of light from my physical heart to break down the obstruction, which was a large stone. As flying debris cleared, a golden light streamed into the dungeon. This began to melt the people and they became silvery-white light, which flowed as a long ribbon, out and up, towards and along a staircase of alabaster steps lined in golden filigree, the symbol of the moment when time and space touch at the centre of the equi-distant crossing point. This is to say symbolically that the cosmic mind level was announcing that a new higher state of consciousness had been achieved.

A moment after this I was back in my body, feeling totally cleansed; but the vision did not end here. At breakfast that morning I began to raise the vibrations in my body to the level of resonance that began to reveal the sacredness of the vision. We left with our guide and to my surprise he took us to St Stephen's Church and the catacombs, which contained the bones of humans, some of them there from ancient times. My dreams were now too becoming metaphors alongside the experience of clairvoyance.

On my return to Austria a year later a friend took us to a concert in a cave outside Vienna. Music floated out of the cave entrance, and I recognized some of the characteristics of the cave as being the same as in the vision with the angel. While the Albanian concert group was taking a break, I asked my friend how the cave and tunnels had been created. He told me that it had been an ancient quarry, and that the Romans had constructed many buildings from the cave rock. It had been used as recently as World War II, but the cave had a history of forced labour and death. The music that emanated from it sounded like the celestial melody from a thousand violins. This was just as I had heard it in the vision, when the music was carried into the heavenly planes, releasing all the human suffering of the past. It is, the Tiwa would say, *through pain that the spirit of trusting returns life to the Golden Light of Truth because pain is the path to Right Actions. We humans who are here now alive on the earth have an opportunity to heal our past lifetimes, and to heal those*

ST STEPHEN'S CHURCH OF THE SACRED 31

lives of our relatives who are no longer with us; as humans we are their reflections therefore connected.

INSIGHT 7: An ancient event or an event in the distant future can be experienced through metaphor in the present.

Practice

The angel is the symbol for light. The bed symbolizes the foundation for life in this context, because the angel is the physical energy vibration of light at the micro-level in the human body, while the bed is the mental placement of consciousness in the person.

In the theme of this chapter I am encouraged by the angel to break free the opening at the end of the cave. The angel is really the light or energy which breaks the cosmic block, which then allows the people who are imprisoned to go free. Remember that 'people' always symbolize vibration, and in this example the stopped flow of cosmic energy.

The word 'angel' contains the A–E vowels. A is the infinite void and E is relativity (all my relations), the grid or web of life. The word 'bed' has the vowel E which is relativity, placement within the divine plan, the web of life. The combination of sounds to use are: A = 'aah'; E = 'eh'; E = 'eh', and together 'aah-eh-eh.' Repeat these sounds silently, practising the steps listed below.

Here is the practice for the reader to try to break mental, emotional, physical or spiritual energy flow blocks.

Step 1   Visualize an angel standing at the foot of your bed, facing you. Focus on a physical, emotional, mental or spiritual energy flow block you would like to remove, visualizing it as blocking the entrance to a cave.

Step 2   Ask the angel to take you to the block; at this point the angel disappears and forms your subsequent actions.

Step 3   Break the block at the imagined entrance with red light that you send from your physical heart. (Red is spiritual light.)

Step 4   Observe the breaking up and removal of the block from the entrance.

Step 5   See a golden light fill the opening to the cave and watch as it melts the suffering people with the vibrations of truth.

Step 6   See a white light fill the area. Take a deep breath and feel the
healing taking place in your body.

In the next story, 'The Pumas', I use the Tiwa metaphors to show you
how I arrive at inner knowing and meaning. And because of this I have
not italicized these metaphors but will let you enjoy them, allowing you
to understand their inner meaning. You will immediately recognize
them because the metaphors in many instances will be poetic.

7 The Pumas

'When you have babies you will have deer meat to eat.'[3] My godfather, Rolando Durand, used to say, 'We eat deer meat so we can always as a people possess great clarity of knowingness.'

'The puma will now come down from the mountain to visit the centre of the people who came from the spirits of the sacred mountains.' These words were told to me by a medicine man weeks before I went hunting in the mountains.

'Let us go up hunting . . .,' Bringer of Knowingness said, speaking in the metaphoric language of my father's people. From this statement I translated the metaphor into the English language in my mind to mean, 'Let us go and hunt the "unborn" or "before thoughtness" and bring it down to the people.' For he was saying that it was '. . . time for endowed purity to beautify the people, to enrich the physical wellness of the people with its powers because soon the sunlight would be further away, as it would be winter.'

He was telling the villagers that deer hunting was a sacred tribal ceremony, and that the deer represented 'the infinite knowing from the beginning'. The act of hunting them brought the vibrancy of the mountain's heart down to the people so that 'the people might again be initiated into great clarity and therefore endow them with miraculous capacities.'

I always said yes to his invitations, because I enjoyed the penetrating spiritual–physical clarity he gave me. The vitality in his motions always awoke images in my mind, and evoked highly imaginative metaphors, giving me great pleasure. Bringer of Knowingness's brother had raised me in his house, and so we belonged to the hunting traditions of the village people. When I answered to 'Let us go up hunting', I said, 'Yes, let's go up . . .', and in metaphor I was saying, 'Let us let the blood flow of awareness . . .', or 'We were born to give our blood totally to the heavenly powers of expansion that will carry us to where the pure light is, from the beginning of awared presence of that place where moment-ness bonded to awareness.' Here I make reference to the powers of the earth that give us the self learning to walk on the good road.

It was the season of *changing leaf*; it was autumn at Picuris Pueblo. 'Eat so that you will not be hungry . . .' his wife instructed us at the early morning breakfast table. I translated her words to mean, 'We were born to eat light [energy], to plant it in ourselves. And to let our bodies be energized for the walking-talking that is initiated for miracles in our destinies.'

By her words she had blessed our deer hunt, and I knew she had given us her lamp so that we might find our way that day. As the significance of her blessing struck me I wanted to shout for joy. A smile came over my face, but at 4am in the dawn light my smile just didn't fit into the other dynamics around our deer hunting preparation. Twice I lowered my face in my attempts to be inconspicuous as I let out short bursts of joyous laughter, and each time she stared at me in confusion. I remembered being in church when the giggles would get started between kneeling and standing, and I recalled my foster father's combi-nation of shock and shame as he looked around to see who might be watching. His words were always the same. 'Be a good little boy' or 'Little growing spirit of Holy Wisdom will not come. Be of the highest resonance', he would whisper, and having said thus would nudge me with his hips so that I fell sideways on the pew. After our commotion he would enjoy a secret smile, as he knew people kneeling immediately around us were quietly admiring him for acting directly on my juvenile irreverence.

I gave Bringer of Knowingness the three eagle feathers which repre-sented the keys to an open path up the mountain (cosmic heart) and to the hunt. Then we were on 'the road', taking 'the heart' direction of those who had lived and followed it before us. We parked the truck next to the US Forest Service line (we were hunting on US forest land). 'Put on your moccasins' he said as we began tying the holy objects, includ-ing pieces of blue corn bread in a cloth, to the belts around our navels, the place of peace as shown by the Belt of Peace worn by the Sowers of Peace. Traditionally hunters did not talk, but walked softly on the skin of the living earth, essence of 'Key' (mother), so when he said 'Put on your moccasins' I heard him saying, 'Become like the reed and let the spirit breath of the Great Mystery wash and purify you, then let your hunting moccasins swallow earth mother's light so that the vibrations of "the people" will walk their songs with you today.' He was blessing me and I knew that the mountain top was the centre, the heart, the path, in metaphor, of the higher self, and that from here we would bring down a blessing for the village people who were waiting below. 'Go call it there' Bringer of Knowingness said, and 'Climb up that pathway' and then he disappeared into the thicket of juniper and willow trees, but his essence still lingered as though it wanted to climb up with me. 'Go call it there' were the blessings of the infinite, of 'without interruption' and of 'unchanging'. 'Give your full living life energy in that direction through your wanderings there, and it will in return let the moments you spent there wash your talk and your walk, so that your walking and talking life will become greater truth.' Walking and talking represent the living spirit of the Earth completing her cycles, and beginning new ones, as karmic vision evolves beyond its own immediate boundaries. And I knew from the Tiwa teachings that winter came into existence from the cold world of the infinite, and that the summer world evolved from the heat of the psychic light, the realm of clairvoyance, mental telepathy, visionary capacities etc.

The wings in flight inside the living breath of the cardiovascular system, the 'Key', the purifier mother, was walking in our physical bodies, our earthly robes, and she was washing our physical and spiritual bodies as we departed into the hunt area. We began climbing high up the Wooden Cross mountain. My foster father took the lower trail to the right and I the upper trail. Two crows, messengers from the infinite void, were flying low, close enough to get a better look, and to scold me for disturbing their spaces. Spaces are the forms, and in this example the crows are the new changes in cosmic thought. They landed nearby, cawed at me a few more times, and then, as if I was no longer a threat to their side of the Wooden Cross, flew on as I watched them. Their mocking sounds grew fainter, and they disappeared like two black dots into the morning sun's rays.

A slow wind gathered down valley and came whirling up the little canyon to where I stood, about three-quarters of the way up the mountain. It was a magical, soft wind, and was swirling gently as if blowing ideas through the pine trees. The sound was like 'wa', as in water, or in Tiwa meaning 'Life'. I imagined that the wind sounds were the meridians for the physical body of the mountain, and that it was the life of the mountain landscape. I had been practising Tai chi for forty-five years, yet I felt I was only just beginning to understand the inner working of the evolution of my spirituality while participating so consciously with the outer landscapes. The concept of Tai chi means the vibration of the cold stream of pure thought of the Higher Mind which is active when you are doing Tai chi because Tai chi is the form of the walking-talking principle. I saw too that the mountain was creating new cloud formations, which I viewed as aspects of the mentality of mind overhead, because there was a cold chill in the air. I stood there for a while, and then I 'sat in stillness' and remembered that 'to sit in stillness' was 'To be washed by the awareness in waiting or by understanding, as in standing under God's wisdom'.

To be totally aware in each moment had been an on-going practice for me, and so I kept close observation of my thoughts and feelings. Just now I began to notice that there seemed to be a special light flowing over everything on the mountain that made me feel as if I was the living essence of time, of forms beyond forms of overlay, that made up all the material forms. I had experienced this sensation before, so I shifted my sitting posture, because I had learned in the past that such a position could produce certain states. I noticed that even after I moved nothing happened. I began to 'walk with more than intense watchfulness', as I wanted to stay in it and to bond to its presence.

I remembered Bringer of Knowingness's wife's blessing words at breakfast, 'Eat so that you will not be hungry.' I knew she had given me her lamp, her light, so that I might see. The shadows of the trees indicated that it was midday on top of Wooden Cross mountain, and I untied the white tea towel containing my blue corn-bread lunch, from around my belt. 'Sit down to eat' was to wash, and plant the self to highest awareness. And then I remembered my wife's words, her voice asking me to return early from the hunt. 'Come home early' translated to, 'while the singing vibrations of the mountain are strong in you, bring them home for us to be nourished by them.' There are ancient stories of hunters travelling away from the heart of the village (universe) so that they could return with new life for the people; the reverse was happening here.

I had barely begun to walk after my meal when I felt I no longer wanted to circle back down the mountain. I was 'deer walking', stepping softly on the skin of the mountain ground cover, channelling the earth light through the soles of my feet, and using it to see. So I became unborn-ness, or of a higher perceptual capacity. And as I fed the deer tracks with the cornmeal, the fresh imprints on the ground returned to me flashes of white light; as they entered my eyes they travelled into my physical body, and washed it from head to toe. Next I dropped some little sparks of lovefulness into them, and danced along up and down between the higher and lower branches of the trees, so as not to miss seeing them. Raising my eyes from the lower to the higher branches connected me to the collective unconscious, whereas the downward motion brought the wisdom of the collective to me. I followed this practice because I wanted to know where the deer were; I could not physically see them, but I could bring them into my consciousness in this way. One might also state that a Tiwa hunter might use this method. When he listened to children's stories he was told that the trees were the symbols of greatness, and that bringing something from the above to the below reveals that which is as yet not known. I had already smelled and tracked the deer's direction. I knew where they were, and that there was a pair, because there were only two sets of fresh tracks.

As I came around a ten-year-old pine tree, concealed beneath its black bark cover, I saw them watching me, waiting for me to shoot one of them. Three days before the hunt in 'a prayer that a deer be given' I had been given permission to slay one. So, at that moment I experienced *déjà vu*, as I had already met them in a clairvoyant experience at the prayer meeting, the 'preparation ceremony'. This would help us to find the path of the deer that had been given to us by the deer spirits.

INSIGHT 8: That one will experience in many instances through ceremonies a moment of clairvoyance: one will see that which one may be seeking at some future time, prior to the moment of encountering it in a physical experience.

My Apache grandfather from Dulce used to say about prayer, 'Prayer is to give the highest goodness the food it needs to stay alive, so that it can elevate itself to its next highest good as it travels within us humans.' Goodness, like us, must be prayed for so that only more good can come to it. Prayers bring heavenly rain droplets of enlightened knowing. Thunder is our mental body aspect. He said that all life was time, and that it was simply passing through the earth and us. Because we are what we eat, we become the power of our eating habits, in how we choose to live both physically and spiritually. He said that in a vision he had learned that the soil on which we live has light-giving qualities, because it is composed of two lights. In each movement that we make a physical flash of speeding light travels endless distances per second in the physical body, but since the body is endless space (forms) it travels, and circles and returns. All things that go out come around, completing cycles. The other light is the spiritual light which has the function of creating indivisibility of unborn-ness. Hence, the two lights that go out return to their origin, leaving new unborn-nesses in their aftermath.

Energy, *wa-chi-chi-hu* as he called it, was an inner living notion of the ability to see the at-one-ment with the All. And in poetry,

When we see light that is emanating from a seed
That moment of insight gives us capacity of All Knowingness
Enshrining anchors it
While the observation of its placement (mirror or reflection)
Gives the ownership of the experience to the perceiver.

INSIGHT 9: As human beings we have an innate sense of knowing that
says that everything we see we automatically own or possess, therefore
we are, by pre-conditioning, territorial. I still think my Apache grandfather was a poet.

The deer was the symbol of this journey of All Knowingness. And
now was the moment to shoot the deer, and it fell. When I walked up to
it a voice spoke as if it was the voice of Clarity, saying 'Feed a very small
amount of "awareness light" into the deer's ear, and do not touch its
body. And leave it lying there.' A strong electromagnetism surrounded
the deer and I, and flooded into my lungs with every breath. It felt like
the shafts of light from the sun that I used to swallow during long vision
quests out in the desert, or at the Southern Ute Sun Dance sunrise
ceremonies. I fed the 'awareness light' into the deer's right ear, and this
action increased the loving, penetrating connection between us. I
walked away, looking back only once; at that moment I did not have
any needs. An hour or so after I left the deer doubt raised its head but it
knew it didn't belong so it left as it had come, quietly. Finally, at about
3pm I reached the starting point of the hunt, where I sat and watched,
and waited for Bringer of Knowingness to return. I began to think of
ways to tell him about my morning experience, and still not reveal the
whole truth, as I didn't want him to know that I had left a deer
unattended up on Wooden Cross mountain. Touching it would have left
the smell of my human presence.

He finally came three hours later. He sat down and said, 'I heard only
one rifle shot from your direction.' And I answered, 'I shot once . . . the
one got away.'

I phrased the answer so that it sounded as if there was only one deer
that had escaped and that there had been only one shot. He didn't seem
to want to continue talking about the hunt, but preferred to share a
hunting experience in the 1930s, when he and my godfather had been
hunting during a cold winter in the Wooden Cross mountain area.

'Your godfather had shot a deer and wounded it. It was running
down the mountainside and right over there we lost the trail of blood
on the snow. Suddenly to our right over here,' he pointed with his right
hand, 'I saw two big shadows moving fast and away from us and they

were gone. We couldn't follow the tracks of the deer any longer because it had got dark, so we went to investigate the sounds coming from the dark shadows, only to find that two adult pumas had left a deer kill, frozen and still half buried in a pile of leaves. They had only eaten the entrails. The meat seemed to be good, so we loaded it on to the back of our mule, and as we were packing it on your godfather joked, "The deer looks like a Wooden Cross riding there on the back of the mule." And we laughed, and then started for home down the trail; it was now getting even darker and only the moonlight kept us on the path. The mule kept moving faster on its way home, and so every now and then it would step on me', and he laughed more at the memory than the humour in it.

Bringer of Knowingness was sharing this story approximately fifty years later, and it didn't seem as though that much time had passed. And as for me telling him about my deer kill I knew by his story that somehow he knew, and chose to respect my privacy.

This deer hunt took place in the autumn of 1979, and on my return that day I said to Red Eagle, my brother, that I had shot a deer, but I was still not capable of telling him the whole story. A week later I flew to Tulsa, Oklahoma, and the people I was visiting drove me up to Independence, Kansas, to do a ceremony. There I met a man who introduced himself, and then said, 'I had a dream vision the other night, and I came all the way from New York especially to meet you, and I was instructed to give you this tan puma paw. I used to live in Taos, New Mexico, and I understand that this puma was killed on your mountain.'

INSIGHT 10: I knew that he was making reference to Picuris mountain, and that he had been sent by the voice that had spoken to me that day while I was standing next to the deer on Wooden Cross mountain. Fifty years later the godson of Roland Duran would return the gift, and leave a deer for the great-grandchildren of the two adult pumas that winter of 1979/80 up on Wooden Cross mountain. It had become the time to return their goodness to the circle of the pumas, that so long ago they had left food for 'the people' of Picuris. In cyclical time all that is created returns eventually to its own original creator; for a moment I was participating in an event that had taken place years before, and I had been chosen to complete a cycle.

Practice

In this context the puma symbolically is visionary capacity, and the deer is all-knowingness.

Step 1   Find a quiet space and relax your mind for a few minutes

Step 2   Imagine a thin curtain or veil in front of you.

Step 3   See a tiny hole in this, which gradually opens and gets bigger.

Step 4   On the other side, you will see a form. Focus on it for a minute or two and see what you can sense or feel from it or about it, and then practise trusting what you receive intuitively.

Use the vowels in puma and deer in order, U—A and E—E (pronounced 'ooo'–'aah'–'eh'–'eh'). Repeat the sounds silently while following the steps.

In the next story, I began to experience the metaphors I had heard in the Picuris children's stories in a real and living way.

8 At the Waterfall

BEFORE I WENT INTO THE WILDERNESS areas hunting for the ancient trails, my father's last blessing was: 'May the spirit of Travelling Paths' caretake your walking talk.' That 'The keepers of clarity, the caretakers of be-ingness and of travels will protect, help and guide you.'

I began to walk along deer trails, following only the map in my head about approximately where the old trail went down to the next town to the north. Somewhere up towards Mora, they had said, but I didn't know for sure.

I stopped after a while and made a ceremony to the trail spirits for their guidance, help and protection. I said: 'I am looking for the Spirit of the Keeper of the Old Trails.' And then I said, 'The little people who have always lived here and to the spirit of Trails spirits.' I asked that a blessing be given me to proceed. 'And I ask too for the blessings from the Spirit of Travelling Paths Who Carries All of Life Here. Only with your full permission can I travel here, therefore, I await your sign. And if it is in your understanding that I cannot travel here I will quickly return to my people.'

A moment passed, and then more stillness, and then another moment when I saw far off, at a place I knew only as beyond the beyond, a leaf. It was very tiny, and then it grew bigger as it came closer and closer. It came fast over into the physical world from the non-physical one, and hit me just above the left eye, before landing gently near my feet, and disappearing. It brought with it the affirmation that I should continue my quest; as the momentary pain on my forehead penetrated slowly it carried with it into my psyche, via my blood, the answer 'yes'. My inner being, delighted, knew my answer had come directly from the world of the spiritual light, of the graciousness of the spirits I had evoked and of the vibration of Trustingness. I had in formal practices been working towards understanding what the energy of trust might feel like. Now it was my time to travel in this space of trusting my walking-talk, because I felt the shift within and knew it was possible, for my travels had been blessed.

Insight 11: Shattering light was in those moments when we are between slices of light, or reading between the gaps that give us insight.

Using the extra earth energy I had gathered into my body while sitting there, I began walking down into the canyon, and soon I came into a dimension of 'time washing' me, as if I was inside a tunnel and being swallowed slowly down into the canyon.

Insight 12: Time washing was the metaphor and the physical experience was the bonding with it. Also it reminded me of when I used to watch the spirit of someone who had just died cross over, and go through the tunnel from the physical world to the spiritual. This phenomenon is, essentially, one of the most important aspects in life, because it defines that space when the old dies and empowers new insight as in the phenomenon of change. Life is continually dying and birthing itself anew. And the walls were cleansing me as I moved towards the sacred direction, because I had been initiated into 'Travelling Paths' by my father. As I moved among the big boulders, the scrub oak, pinon and juniper trees, I sensed the watchful presence of caretakers of the geographical area.

My father instructed me to 'Listen to what the elders of the Spirit World tell you.' He further said, 'Advice Giver' came into being when the action of 'doing' 'became'. It augmented the expansion of the self from the relative to the greater absolute.

Recalling my recent experience with the leaf I remembered that many times as a boy I played the ancient game of 'dropping leaves', and watched them drifting to the Earth. I used to wait in a clearing down by the river and look for the falling cottonwood leaves, and I used to run to one and catch it in my left hand. I would run with it in my palm until I could no longer feel its cool *chi* (cold truth) penetrating my hand. And as I ran I used to watch the *chi* climbing inside the bone marrow up my left arm and into my head. And I used to imagine the leaves were returning back up the branches of the cottonwood tree whence they had come. The sensations of playing this game always cooled my head and clarified my thoughts. Now I was imagining that I was inside the tunnel, and I felt that I could physically feel the *chi*, its 'Invigorating Truth Serum', slipping out of the walls and into me and I melting into the coolness of my brain. I realized then that I was in a state free of earthly duality. Hence I had powers of miraculous proportions.

Along a small stream I saw fish with big heads and small bodies, either malnourished, or quite primitive. The bottom of the canyon was so thick with fallen trees that at times I crawled in between the logs and branches, just to slide through and keep moving down in the direction of the stream flow.

I found fresh deer, puma, rabbit and coyote tracks, and lots of squirrels living in this hidden valley.

INSIGHT 13: The deer means to name knowingness; puma, to have visionary capacities; rabbit, to be higher states of cosmic healing; coyote, to move upwards and onwards along the cosmic grid; and squirrels, to evolve beyond self-imposed limitations. I tried reasoning that this place was in another dimension, or else it was so secluded that not a single human soul had ever been here. At one point I felt a phantom hunger which meant to me to 'die into passivity and not to question', and I knew too that in order to satisfy the physical hunger I could just breathe in the atmospheric canyon air. I did and it worked! In awe I attempted to breath the particles of air light again and again. Later as I thought about the experience I realized that these foods were the essence of the principles that had come into being in the early dawn of time and were the first ideas that made up the territory of the meta-phoric mind today. Food made up of the spiritual breath of the Mother–Father for their children of the living earth, a gift the Great Mystery had left for the ever-blooming flower, the planet Earth. And then there were my tears that came out of thanksgiving. For I had been taken back to that time before the passions that kept me in dualism had first appeared.

INSIGHT 14: I understood that there are six passions capable of keeping us from our insightful capacities if we allow them to rule us. They are attachment, jealousy, pride, greed, anger and mental obscur-ation. However, I found that if I could use these passions creatively I could go beyond them to my true nature of staying wide awake and receptive to new insights.

What I was experiencing was the original dream of what is-ness is! And how Planting Mother originally gave us our placement, and that the dream is an action that for all of the eternities is to be carried by us. And we 'the people' (vibrations) are the actions of our Mother–Father's dreams. We are the physical velocity of their light, and through our earthly robe, the flesh that houses the spirit of the living essences of 'wa', they can participate in the indivisibility of the illuminations of the primary intelligence as light within us.

I was walking on a trail in semi-darkness, and only occasionally a shaft of light came through the trees. And then up ahead I saw a clearing where the light was everywhere. As I approached it I felt a warming breeze emanating from it: the mid-afternoon sunlight. As I entered the clearing, the stream I had been following disappeared into the earth to my right. As I walked another 10 to 15 feet forward towards the edge, I heard the first sound of the waterfall, descending to a strata of ancient stones far below.

Stepping cautiously, I walked up to the rim of the cliff, and looked down the streams of falling water. There were rainbows dancing over the dropping water, and the wind was fanning out beautifully coloured sprays. I sat to watch, to rest and to ponder how I would continue my walk along the stream bed since it was now 200 feet below me. I thought, 'To climb up the canyon will take me a day, and to scale the canyon walls down to the lower level of the stream bed is an impossibility.' I didn't know what to do, so I sat quietly and began drinking the rainbow in with my eyes, and the vision calmed my fears. I remembered the original idea of the Magpietail Boy myth (see page 58) in which the wizards made rainbows with parts of their bodies. I sat and, 'stopping the breath', began to relax so that the spirits of this place might assist me in my dilemma. I knew how to listen respectfully to the elders; like me, they were the vibrations of the living earth.

The ever-changing rainbows made my eyes heavy, so after a while I closed them slowly. Then, as I enjoyed the peace around me, a gentle voice came from behind, saying 'See, there behind you is a 10-foot pole. Take it, scale the cliff wall to your left. Do it now, and we will help you along the wall.' I turned very slowly, because I wasn't sure that I really was hearing a voice. As I opened my eyes, part of me wanted to see who was talking, but the other part of me did not. I compromised, and turned very slowly, but I saw no one. However, there on the ground behind me was a wooden pole, and it was 10 feet long.

I got up, picked up the pole and began to scale the 200-foot walls of the canyon, remembering that the walls in the dreaming landscape belong to the yellow butterflies or spiritual gold.

INSIGHT 15: We scale the walls of our own unclarities, and in so doing give direction to the evolutionary progress of culture, to the advancement of human life on the Earth.

I imagined myself immersed in the yellow gold openness of truth butterflies, which I was seeing in metaphor, and descended one step at a time. And I remembered my father's blessings of help, protection and guidance. I just knew too that the elders, my spiritual helpers, were my companions on this first solo flight on the slippery canyon wall with my 10-foot pole.

I held onto the cliff wall with my left hand, and with my right held the pole and used it to find a firm hold on the cliff ledge, while I inched my feet along. Every time I found a new place for the pole it seemed to become anchored in position by a gentle force, like a warm wind, enabling me to steady myself while I found a new secure foothold.

After a while I reached a ledge some 20 feet from the bottom of the cliff, where I dropped the pole and jumped down onto a pile of broken shale, which instantly began to slip down. So I ran as fast as I could, knowing that I was descending the mountainside at a rate of 10 to 15 feet with each step. I grabbed on to a small pinon tree that was partially uprooted. It began to give, but it held my weight while I grabbed for – and missed – the top of a tall spruce tree that reached up above the canyon's edge. I tried to grasp the spruce again, but I realized that to do so I would have to let go of the pinon and trust. I fell upon the top of the spruce, and for a moment I moved beyond my self-imposed limitations and felt like a squirrel, flopping and swaying on a tree branch. I could smell the scent of the spruce, and could sense that the sticky sap had glued my hands into a tight hold. The wind blew, cooling the sweat on my brow, that I had only just begun to notice. Below me the rock slide had created a choking brown dust that was rising all around me. I sat on the tree top and waited for the dust to settle, and then lowered myself on to a firmer branch and drank in the energy of the spruce. It cleared and strengthened my lungs. And then I remembered again the Picuris' children's story of Magpietail Boy, and how Elf Boy had helped him, and how he had descended the spruce tree to the bottom of the cliff walls.

INSIGHT 16: I had just experienced some of the metaphors in the story. I had jumped and slipped 75 feet down a cliff wall, and could not help but see the similarities between my experiences and those of Magpietail Boy.

Later, as I climbed down the tree and returned to my car, I recognized a different clarity both in me and in my surroundings. It was as if I was 'metaphor alongside experience', and that the trees, grasses and the flowing stream were physically affirming and lovingly reconciling my experiences. I could sense the true nature of life.

INSIGHT 17: As I walked home down the canyon trail I realized that I could only absorb the teachings I had received at the waterfall through physical actions, drink them into my soul and then fully integrate them by walking and talking about my experiences.

When I reached my car I turned and looked back up into the canyon. There was a mountain between me and the waterfall, but for a moment I

was able to see the waterfall through the solid mass; suddenly I had a visual ability to see through objects, and that realization filled me with surprise and astonishment. The Be-ing of Insights always seems to surprise the Be-ing of Believing We Exist in this manner. I then drove home.

I also remembered another visionary experience, when I had the ability to see for hundreds and thousands of miles into the starry night sky, simply using my physical eyes. Again I was surprised that I could do this, and then I had an insight that the Be-ing of True Potential Possibilities lives in the moment of surprise in which all humans can participate when they are in well-integrated self-actualized states.

A week after my experiences at the waterfall I travelled to Virginia Beach where I gave a talk to a group of psychology students. I told of my adventures, and after my lecture a young woman asked me if I read minds. Jokingly I answered 'Yes, sometimes', and then asked 'Why?' She said, 'Because you have just told my dream. *You see,' she said, 'I was the person scaling the canyon walls and you told the dream exactly as I dreamt it a week ago.'*

INSIGHT 18: There must be only one true reality, and that is all taking place within the reality of *The One Great Mystery*, called 'Light of Living Truth'.

So that for her and for me, for a moment, we became one, in the one Great Mystery. I was her dream, and she was my experience.

Practice

In 'At the Waterfall' the 'water' symbolizes 'life', and the 'fall' represents the relationship with friends, relatives or situations.

The vowel sounds of the word 'waterfall' are A–E–A, pronounced 'aah'–'eh'–'aah'.

Step 1   Find a meditation posture comfortable for you.

Step 2   Repeat the 'aah'–'eh'–'aah' sound vibrations silently.

Step 3   While holding the image of the waterfall in your mind's eye begin to send the 'life' (healing light) of the water to a friend, relative or situation.

9   The Journey with the Mermen

Symbolically speaking, doors open for us in their own time. There is a right time for doors to open because time has to do with the action of doing, such as opening the door for action to take place.

Harmony is the state of being receptive to the embraces of life. Harmony was the being created by Ocia-o-ney, the 'Birther of Babies', the spirit present along with the midwife when Tiwa babies are born. This also applies to the birthing of ideas, as in cognizance. The Greeks called him Oceanus, creator spirit of the ocean of cosmic thought. The Greeks also believed that Oceanus entered the ocean of cosmic thought to weave us into his dreams, and that today he lies there, dreaming us awake. When the Mermen of the sea called for my help in healing the pollution of Oceanus' domain they taught me a fire ceremony for healing my inner and outer landscapes. It all began in Marin County, California, in 1984.

We left San Francisco with a plan to perform ceremonies high up on the cliffs above the sea in Marin County. While travelling up to the mountain top I thought of 'standing awareness' and of how the good in goodness stands always at the centre of the inner landscape in life. And had we not travelled up to its topmost point of reference? Later on that day at the sweat lodge (an ancient purification ritual) the people involved in the ceremony became 'the essence of the rearrangement of the disarray of life that is in perpetual change'.

INSIGHT 19: To sweat is to transcend duality. The earth was the self as the ever-unfolding flower and we, her children, were evolving with her. I knew too that periodically we rearrange our musical vibrations as we tune our forms to higher levels of our newly found songs or ways. Long ago we learned from story tellers that we the people had come to live with 'changing woman', and so the earth plane was made 'of the house that shatters' and that we were of those vibrations. Three events happened at the sweat lodge ceremony. The first one was 'to open the door', the second was 'the lights in the body', and the third was 'down the cliff wall to the ocean'. The first, 'to open the door', is the metaphor that allows us to enter into each moment without any direction on our part. The second event came as 'pricking, like thousand upon thousand of tiny needles, on my skin, as lights that appeared as if I was gazing into a starry night'.

INSIGHT 20: In my physical body each light was a biological cell and there were so many of them. In another instant as I was lying there in the oscillation of the body lights, first one, and then another, and still a third one appeared. They were Mermen, fishmen of the sea.

The Mermen were the original beings who came from outer space, *Kua-ouu-teh*, and brought civility to the Earth. They lived in the oceans by night, and in the daylight came to teach about respect for life. Standing before me they seemed to be made of golden light. Above their waists they had beautifully built masculine bodies, and below they had fish tails, but at a closer look I could see that they stood on two human feet. The first one spoke. 'We have to take you to the one who wants to see you', which meant new changes or cycles were beginning. Before I could respond all three turned and dived down the side of the high rock cliffs, and with the shocking force of their departure I was pulled downwards behind them. As I was jerked out of my physical body, my astral body observed that my muscles were still in a state of re-orientation, and I felt awkward as I went down the cliff walls. And so came the third event: 'The self was a growing harmonic force of the flower of the ever greater light.' I understood at that moment the words, 'In every single moment of life we are given the opportunity to live, in each one we are enshrined with the graciousness of the ever-present which means the Earth is "the higher soul self that is moving presently to its highest good".'

As I was falling I saw all three of them break the ocean blue, leaving white circles of foam behind them. Then I was swimming inside a tunnel underneath the ocean floor, and the three Mermen were in front of me. 'The tunnel journey' was to me 'to awaken a higher physical–spiritual consciousness. The tunnel journey energy-shifts from the physical body to the spiritual body, and to a lesser degree shifts too in the emotional and mental bodies.' And I knew that the hundreds of lights emanating from the tunnel walls were shooting lifelines for my inner awakening.

New assignments come as we grow out of old ones, and next I found my consciousness standing in front of the Merman King, who was sitting on a throne in the middle of a large cavern. He was cloaked in an ocean-blue cape that was resonating all the colours of the rainbow. He looked exactly like the be-ing of universal harmony in the Picuris children's stories, and in mental telepathy he communicated to me my new assignment, which was to heal my personal confusion with sacred fires, and by so doing I could heal that of the physical worlds. The exquisite stones of sapphires, of emeralds, of diamonds on this jewel-studded throne were the metaphors for the new revelations that were 'all ready' to appear in both the cosmic and physical worlds. With his mind he shot a light about two feet above the ground in front of me, and this time he spoke with his whole body and said, 'The sacred fire, and reflections of the flames on the walls of the sacred sound chambers, will bring the life force to the roots of peace lights on earth.' And he said furthermore, 'The light flames of your fires on the chamber walls will reflect away the dark pollution on the dark walls, the unclarities of the self at the micro as well as at the macro level, of the self, and that of the dark cosmic ocean. And do a fire ceremony on 7 April and on each seventh of every month thereafter.'

INSIGHT 21: Seven meant for me 'a new path', and that if I wanted to have new insights, I could build a fire every seventh of the month to ensure continuity of insight.

The vision was gone. I was struggling to re-enter my body, only to be awakened by a friend who I had seen in New Mexico only a week before, and he had lost his way at night. He said: 'I saw your light in the darkness of the night and I came to ask for directions. I had been thinking of you all evening, and for some unknown reason I chose to wander out of the city and up in this direction. I was lonely for your good fellowship and counselling. And here you are!' Touching his forehead he said, 'I can't believe this is actually happening', and he began to help us take down the sweat lodge. And in metaphor, friendship is the way of the expansion of the inner and outer truth. Friendships are forever and if there are changes when friends separate, stillness holds their friendship in a state of Loving Purity regardless.

That very same day I cancelled all my lectures and appointments in California and left for New Mexico to do the purification fires for the Merman King.

In Bernalillo, New Mexico, at 11.30pm on the night of 7 April, 1984, we built the first holy fire in the chamber of the sacred sounds. As the embers slowly died away, to my surprise I saw many faces in the dying embers which represented blocked mental, emotional and spiritual energies in the psyche of cosmic consciousness. They were in the process of releasing their hold on the physical level and transcending their fiery forms beyond the level of physical reality. We continued to build six other purification fires in the chamber, and for the last one we travelled to Colorado. While driving there I saw a shark swimming across and in front of our car in a vision. Pictures were taken of the last purification fire, and when we had them developed a week later, we found in one a beautiful shark in the background. A week later a friend, a male nurse from one of the Santa Fe hospitals, came to our house and showed us a photo of a petroglyph of a fish that he had taken on a visit to one of the national monuments in southern New Mexico. And when I saw it, standing above the eyes of the fish was the image or figure of a tiny Merman.

And I learned that same week that around four hundred years ago the people who lived in what is now the Coronado State Park Monument (which is geographically one mile from Oceanus' first sound chamber in Bernalillo, New Mexico) were a Fish (water) Society, and they were Tiwas linguistically.

INSIGHT 22: Apparently, by living and staying focused in the medium of our talents, our innate intelligence through metaphor alongside experience keeps our physical body connected to enlightenment.

Also, during the vision when I was taken into the sky I went into thick dark rain clouds, that were lying over my home and were 20,000 feet in the sky. They were part of the clouds that come into New Mexico across the vast expanse from the Pacific (Peace) Ocean, or the regions of Marin County, California. These weather storms are carried by the prevailing winds across the United States. I found myself again in a vision, standing before a ring of elders who were in ceremonial dress with their blankets. I knew then that the Merman King, the Bernalillo sound chamber and the Fish Society were all connected. 'Why have you not built the sound chamber?' asked one of the elders. 'Because I have not been able to find a place to build it,' was my response. Then the answer came back from the same elder, 'We will show you where to build it', and in the next instant I was standing outside in my garden, and the elders became an oval of light and descended to the ground. Moments later, a second ring of light descended and inside it was an angel with beautiful long, silvery wings, carrying a baby in its arms, and as it placed it onto the ground it said, 'You must raise this child.' Next I found myself back in my body in the sweat lodge where I had been leading the ceremony. That same evening, before the potluck feast which follows all such ceremonies, I announced to the people that I was

going to build the sound chamber there in my garden, and I shared with
them the vision I had just received.

I began to build it the very next day, by designating the foundation
with my roto-tiller. It was in October 1983 and on 1 January, 1984, we
dedicated it.

To the reader: If Ocia-o-ney means 'Birther of Babies or Ideas', the
fact that the chamber was given to the world from the Pacific Ocean,
which means peace, perhaps means that Oceanus was telling us that a
new idea for world peace was given to the world in that moment.

INSIGHT 23: At the time of writing the child that was given to the
Earth in metaphor is nine years old. And as of this writing, there are
twenty-one Peace Chambers around the world, waiting for the time
when the child is old enough to start teaching us about the sounds of
world peace.

**Practice
for achieving Mental–Emotional Balance**

In the Mermen, the E–E (relativity/relativity) vowels, and the sound vibration of 'eh'–'eh', are in use. The Mermen in this context represent symbolically the balance of mental and emotional equilibrium.

Step 1   Get into a comfortable meditative position.

Step 2   Repeat the 'eh'–'eh' sounds silently.

Step 3   Visualize a weighing scale in front of you.

Step 4   On the left side of the scale see a round sphere labelled 'Feelings', and on the right side one labelled 'Senses'.

Step 5   Begin giving light energy to the side of the scale that has less energy until such time as the two scales are balanced.

Allow four days for the balance between your emotional and mental states to be reached. Feelings are the same as emotions, and mental states the same as sensations.

Now follows the Picuris children's story that I introduced at the beginning of the book. Please enjoy reading it just as it is. In the second version (page 61), I have translated the meaning of the metaphors. Please understand that the story has multiple meaning so that the translations that I present are only at one level. Perhaps you may want to try to find others. In any case, enjoy it!

PART TWO

10 Magpietail Boy and his Wife

LONG, LONG, LONG AGO THE PEOPLE were living at Picuris Pueblo. And Magpietail Boy and his wife, Yellow Corn Woman, lived there. Yellow Corn Woman belonged to the Society of Wizards, and she used to go every night, as soon as it got dark, to where the Wizards were doing their sacred ceremonies. Magpietail Boy liked to sleep so much that he did not know where his wife went in the evenings, nor at what time of night she came back. Sometimes she would come home before midnight, and sometimes she would return by early morning light. But her husband, Magpietail Boy, was such a sleepyhead that he did not know where she had been.

Then one day he said to himself, 'Suppose I do not sleep tonight. When I lie down in bed this evening I will close my eyes and pretend to be asleep. And as soon as she goes I will follow her to see where she goes every night.'

And that night, after she had given him his supper, she said, 'My husband, you must lie down now, for it is time for you to sleep.' Magpietail Boy pretended that he was very tired and said, 'All right, I am really sleepy, so I will lie down.' And then he lay down and, pretending that he was asleep, began to snore.

Yellow Corn Woman began to get ready to leave when suddenly somebody was at the door. She went to the door and Magpietail Boy heard someone saying, 'Hurry, you are already late.' Magpietail Boy recognized the voice, and said to himself, 'My wife has been doing ceremonies with the Wizards, so I will follow her.' Yellow Corn Woman, wearing her ceremonial clothes, left the house. As soon as she was gone, Magpietail Boy got up, dressed, and followed her along the trail. Because the moon was shining on her moccasins they looked white like snow. Magpietail Boy watched his wife enter the chamber of the

Wizards, so he knew where she was every night . . . performing ceremonies with the Wizards! He hid by the chamber roof-hole, concealing himself behind the roof-hole poles.

As he looked down into the chamber the Wizards began to prepare themselves. Some took their eyes out; some cut their noses off, or their ears, or their legs, and some cut themselves exactly in half. They were all fixing themselves in various ways. After they had finished dressing, the leader said, 'Let us start', and as he did so the Wizards made a rainbow that crossed the room. Then they began the ceremony, but when they tried to climb the rainbow, they kept falling down. The leader said, 'I believe there is a person here around us who is not with us,' and he sent one of the Wizards out to look. The Wizard searched among the bushes and about the chamber, but could not find anyone, so he returned to the chamber and said, 'There is no one outside.'

Again they started their ceremony and tried to climb the rainbow but kept falling back. 'Stop,' said the leader. 'There must be someone who is not with us. This is why we are failing in our ceremony. Suppose we call the Grass Owl, who can see in the dark.' So they asked the Grass Owl for assistance. 'Oh, Grass Owl, because you can see in the dark we ask your help. There is someone not with us near here, which is why our ceremony is failing. So that is why we are asking you to help us.' 'Hu, hu,' said the Grass Owl and then he went flying outside. He searched around in the weeds and in the bushes but he did not find anyone. However, as he was returning to the chamber his keen eyes caught sight of the tail of a wolf emerging from the roof-hole poles. He said to the Wizards, 'Hu, hu. I did not find anyone outside, but there is a wolf-skin tail sticking out from the roof-hole,' and saying 'Hu, hu,' he flew away.

Yellow Corn Woman knew who it was right away, and she said to herself, 'That must be my husband.' 'Let one of you go and bring him in, whoever it is who is out there,' said the Head Wizard. And as one of the Wizards looked about at the chamber entrance he found Magpietail Boy, and brought him down into the room where the leader said, 'How come you are in my territory?' But Magpietail Boy did not answer. He was then taken to where his wife was seated. Since it was after midnight, he could hardly keep his eyes open, so he laid his head on Yellow Corn Woman's lap and fell to sleep. When the Wizards had completed their ceremony, they created a cliff bench in the canyon and Magpietail Boy was put there while he slept.

When he awoke, quite early the next morning, he found himself lying face up on the cliff bench. 'How am I going to get out of here?' he said. It was impossible for him to move or to turn over, since the bench was only just wide enough for him, and he could only look upward.

It just so happened that Elf Boy lived nearby. 'I believe I will go for a walk down south-west to the river today,' he said as he started out along the trail to the river. Singing as he went, he passed right by where Magpietail Boy was lying, and Magpietail Boy called from below, 'Whoever you are, please stop and help me get out of this place.' Elf Boy heard the call and went to look, and saw Magpietail Boy lying on his back on the cliff bench. 'Ah, Magpietail Boy, is that you?' Magpietail Boy said, 'Elf Boy, please get me out of here.' 'Please wait, because I am on my way to the river, to Fish Maiden, but I will return shortly,' said Elf Boy. Then Elf Boy went to the river.

He found Fish Maiden relaxing by the water. 'Good morning, Fish Maiden,' he said. Elf Boy went over to where Fish Maiden was drying and her mouth was beginning to open. 'I must return to the water as I have been out too long.' Elf Boy said, 'Could you wait a while longer?' Fish Maiden replied, 'I cannot stay out of the water for very long,' which made Elf Boy angry.

On his way back, he picked five cones from a tall spruce tree, and took them to where Magpietail Boy was stuck on the cliff. Elf Boy said, 'I will help you to get out of here, if you will catch but one of these five spruce cones. I am going to drop one at a time and if you miss them, you will not be able to get out.' 'Very well, I will try to catch them.' Then Elf Boy dropped one of them, but Magpietail Boy missed it. He dropped him another one, but still Magpietail Boy did not catch it. Now Elf Boy scared him by saying, 'You must catch this one because it is the last.' 'Yes, I will catch it,' said Magpietail Boy, but he missed it as well. 'Well then, I suppose you will just have to stay up there as that is all I had,' Elf Boy said. Magpietail Boy said nothing, but Elf Boy could see that he was beginning to look very frightened. Then Elf Boy took out another spruce cone. 'Now, this time I am telling you it is the last one, and if you do not catch it, I cannot help you get out of here.' As Elf Boy spoke he dropped the cone and Magpietail Boy reached out and caught it. 'All right,' Elf Boy said. 'Drop the cone and let it fall straight down.' He followed these instructions, and when the cone hit the ground a spruce tree grew up beside him next to the cliff. 'Now, you can climb up the spruce tree.' With a sigh of relief Magpietail Boy did so. 'Thank you for your help,' he said, and then he told Elf Boy the whole story of what had happened to him. 'Very well,' said Elf Boy, leading him over to a fallen tree. Elf Boy picked out a woodworm and gave it to Magpietail Boy, and told him, 'You must place this worm by Yellow Corn Woman's bed.

When you get home, do not tell her what you are doing, and you must not quarrel with her.' Elf Boy then went home.

When Magpietail Boy got home, he sat awhile. Yellow Corn Woman gave him something to eat, and then they both went to bed. Magpietail Boy put the worm next to where Yellow Corn Woman slept, and it entered her navel that night while she was asleep. The worm ate up all her entrails and Yellow Corn Woman died. And so Magpietail Boy lived happily ever after, alone.

And now you have a tale.

In this second writing of the Magpietail Boy story, I have translated one of the levels of meaning, so enjoy reading it again for the deeper content of meaning.

11   Magpietail Boy and his Wife Explained

I LISTENED TO THE PICURIS STORY TELLERS relating the tale of Magpietail Boy and his wife every winter for twenty years. It helped me to develop my visionary capacities further because the story teaches which qualities in life must be cultivated should one desire the life of the mystic. This development was instrumental in my awakening to life's wonders and beauties, and I will outline these qualities in each line of the myth of Magpietail Boy and his Wife.

I think this myth is about God's first attempts at creating what is now considered the cosmos. Out of this story came all of the archetypes that later became cosmic consciousness.

'Long, long, long ago the people were living at Picuris Pueblo' means that the original people (meaning 'vibration') came from Sand Lake, and that each tiny particle of sand in Sand Lake can be seen as an opportunity for insight. This first line of the story refers to the fact that each moment is connected to a vast intelligence, because each tiny sand particle is a moment of insight connected to all the billions and billions of experiences that we, as human beings, have access to. Sand Lake is the metaphor for the cosmos; furthermore, that Picuris Pueblo makes reference to it being the centre of the universe, the heart of the Picuris Pueblo world-view. 'Magpietail Boy' means that if we are not in Awakened Awareness we may veer away from the insight. 'Yellow Corn Woman' means to enter into awareness. 'And Magpietail Boy and his wife, Yellow Corn Woman, lived there' means to live one's life in total awareness so that one may be open to new ideas, to accept them into one's life and to manifest them.

'Yellow Corn Woman belonged to the Society of Wizards' means to be open to healing awareness which emanates from new ideas, or new forms, so that physical stagnation does not occur. 'Yellow Corn Woman used to go every night to where the Wizards were doing their sacred ceremonies.' 'Yellow Corn Woman used to go every night' means to be receptive to new understanding, however it presents itself. 'To where the Wizards were doing their sacred ceremonies' means that psychic healing occurs automatically for anyone who is open to new awareness, because this has a healing effect when it is integrated into the psyche. 'Magpietail Boy liked to sleep so much that he did not know where his wife went in the evenings, nor at what time of the night she came back' means that there are two ways in which we can live our lives. One is to wander aimlessly (asleep), believing we exist, and the other is to live life in a state of conscious awareness. Our greatest challenge is to maintain a conscious, awakened awareness because there is always a possibility of falling asleep while believing that one is consciously awake and connected to metaphor. 'As soon as it got dark, Yellow Corn Woman used to go over to where the Wizards had their sacred ceremonies' means that awareness, and therefore insight, cannot take place if one is asleep. 'Sometimes she would come home before midnight, and sometimes she would come home by early morning light' means that half measures in life will achieve nothing. 'And sometimes she would come home by early morning light' means that Magpietail Boy needed to be awakened and initiated to arouse his awareness. 'But her husband, Magpietail Boy, was a sleepyhead so that he did not know where she had been every night' means that he was in a state of non-awareness, asleep.

'Then one day he said to himself, "Suppose I do not sleep tonight, so that I will know where my wife goes every night" ' means that now he was alert to insight in each moment that one lives. 'Tonight I will follow her and when I lie down in bed this evening I will close my eyes and pretend to be asleep' means that one must begin at the foundation of one's life and start to seek higher awareness. 'And as soon as she goes I will follow her to see where she goes every night' means to cultivate opportunities in life by following them, completing them and totally integrating them into one's existence.

'And then one night, after she had given him his supper, she said, "My husband, you must lie down now, for it is time for you to sleep" ' means that there is a tendency in life to regress to earlier habits. And also that the very qualities that awaken us in life paradoxically have the power to put us back to sleep. Why? Because to be clear about the direction one wants to take requires effort. 'Magpietail Boy pretended that he was very sleepy and said, "All right, I am really tired, so I will lie down," ' means that he has decided to become awakened and aware. 'And then he lay down and, pretending that he was asleep, began to snore.'

'Yellow Corn Woman began to get ready to leave when suddenly somebody was at the door. She went to the door and Magpietail Boy heard someone saying, "Hurry, you are already late" ' means that in order for one to be in a state of total wakefulness, one must be open to the unexpected, as in insight. 'Magpietail Boy recognized the voice' means to stay mentally and physically alert. 'And said to himself, "My wife has been doing ceremonies with the Wizards, so I will follow her" ' means to follow the openness to insight as the path to awareness. 'Yellow Corn Woman, wearing her ceremonial clothes, left the house' means the expression of one's core beliefs must be flexible enough so that new understanding can be assimilated without the least hesitation. 'As soon as she was gone, Magpietail Boy got up, dressed, and followed her' means that Magpietail Boy decides to follow the path that will lead him to his highest achievements in life.

'Yellow Corn Woman went out and along the trail' refers to the path of awakened awareness. 'Because the moon was shining on her moccasins they looked white like snow, as she went to the chamber of the Wizards' means that the physical body experience must merge with metaphor. 'Magpietail Boy watched his wife enter' means that a connection is made between the physical and the spiritual worlds, in order to connect the inner consciousness of the individual to cosmic consciousness. 'And so he knew where she was every night . . . performing ceremonies with the Wizards!' means that healing takes place when the inner awareness and cosmic awareness are connected. 'He hid by the chamber roof-hole, concealing himself behind the roof-hole poles' means constant vigilance is necessary so that one is ready to experience only that which can come from the highest greatness.

'As he looked down into the chamber the Wizards began to prepare themselves' means healing begins at the centre of the physical heart, where lies the centre of the cosmic heart, and expands from there to the peripheries of the cosmic universe. 'Some took their eyes out' means cultivating insight by studying and going beyond polarities we find in life; 'some cut their noses off' means expanding awareness; 'some cut their ears off' means that work or intentional suffering was seen as a gift of life for finding insight; 'some cut their legs off' means reconciliation of polarities, seen as the direction of life; 'and some cut themselves exactly in half' means half measures avail us nothing, or that fear of the loss of physical existence also can bring forth insights. 'They were all fixing themselves in various ways' means metaphor alongside experience is what carries life. 'After they had finished dressing, the leader said, "Let us start", and as he did so the Wizards made a rainbow that crossed the room' means physical energy is the connection to insight. 'Then they began the ceremony' means that it is through the physical body that we can catch the metaphors of Awakened Awareness. 'When they tried to climb the rainbow, they kept falling down' means that the art of insight requires effort. 'Their leader said, "I believe there is a person here around us who is not with us" ' means that insight has no form of its own, but that it comes out of its hiding place of the moment. 'And he sent one of the Wizards out to look. The Wizard searched among the bushes and about the chamber, but could not find anyone, so he returned to the chamber and said "There is no one outside". This means that the moment is created because it then becomes the place in which to search for insight in life.

'Again they started their ceremony and tried to climb the rainbow but kept falling back. "Stop," said the leader. "There must be someone who is not with us. This is why we are failing in our ceremony. Suppose we call the Grass Owl, who can see in the dark." So they asked the Grass Owl for assistance. "Oh, Grass Owl, because you can see in the dark we ask your help. There is someone not with us near here, which is why our ceremony is failing. So that is why we are asking you to help us." ' The grass owl is the symbol of ancient wisdom. ' "Hu, hu," said the Grass Owl and then he went flying outside.' The owl, when saying 'Hu', is indicating that insight is what carries the meaning of life, and that metaphor alongside experience are the tools required to perpetuate life unfolding upon life. 'He searched around in the weeds and in the bushes but he did not find anyone' means that insight must start at the physical body. 'However, as he was returning to the chamber' means to work always from the place of integrity. 'His keen eyes caught sight of the tail of a wolf emerging from the roof-hole poles' means that relativity comes into being and the idea that 'all my relations' and everything thereafter would be interrelated. 'He said to the Wizards, "Hu, hu. I did not find anyone outside, but there is a wolf-skin tail sticking out from the roof-hole," and saying "Hu, hu," he flew away.' At this moment the owl is saying that cosmic relativity or human relations are connected through the principle of perfection, meaning that in the physical world human relationships would be a never-ending struggle because each moment has its own balances or imbalances.

'Yellow Corn Woman knew who it was right away, and she said to herself, "That must be my husband." "Let one of you go and bring him in, whoever it is who is out there," said the Head Wizard. And as one of the Wizards looked about at the chamber entrance he found Magpietail Boy, and brought him down into the room where the leader said, "How come you are in my territory?" ' 'Found Magpietail Boy and brought him down into the room' presents the idea of initiation, that all forms in life would have to go through an initiation thereafter. The owl is the symbol of the dreamtime, and the weeds and bushes are symbols of the chaos within the dreamtime. The stepladder which is used to bring Magpietail down into the chamber is the symbol of the Christian cross, or relativity versus the grid; the chamber is the metaphor for the personal or universal self. 'But Magpietail Boy did not answer' means tuning the physical body so that it can experience the vibration of insight. 'He was then taken to where his wife was seated.' For the first time we have the principle of transcendence. 'Since it was after midnight, he could hardly keep his eyes open' means the keys to the doors of life are metaphors. 'So he laid his head on Yellow Corn Woman's lap and fell to sleep' means that life's direction is pre-destined; Believing We Exist falls asleep and merges into Awakened Awareness falling. When the Wizards had completed their ceremony, they created a cliff ledge in the arroyo. Magpietail Boy was laid horizontally on it while he was asleep. As soon as this happens the horizontal continuum is introduced for the first time. And now we have the vertical and the horizontal as forms of inner action that make up the essential form of the grid in consciousness.

'When he awoke, quite early the next morning, he found himself lying face up on the cliff bench', means that higher consciousness and life are always moving upwards, and that cultural evolution is born. ' "How am I going to get out of here?" he said. It was impossible for him to move or to turn over, since the bench was only just wide enough for him, and he could only look upward.' At this point the horizontal aspect of the continuum of consciousness is seeking for ways to fulfil its destiny, and that is the interpretation of the line 'How am I going to get out of here' – that culture is what creates evolution in mankind.

'It just so happened that Elf Boy lived nearby' means the contrast between shadow and light, polarities, duality and reflection; the way to the achievement of higher consciousness. ' "I believe I will go for a walk down south-west to the river today," ' means that at this point we are introduced to linear thought. 'He said as he started out along the trail to the river' means that we now have the principle of forgetfulness at play in seeking insight. 'Singing as he went, he passed right by where Magpietail Boy was lying' means the here and now is created, 'and Magpietail Boy called from below, "Whoever you are, please stop and help me get out of this place" ' means that only in the present can life grow or consciousness evolve because the past has already gone and the future has not yet arrived. 'Elf Boy heard the call and went to look, and he saw Magpietail Boy lying on his back on the cliff bench. "Ah, Magpietail Boy, is that you?" Magpietail Boy said, "Elf Boy, please get me out of here." "Please wait, because I am on my way to the river, to Fish Maiden, but I will return shortly," said Elf Boy. Then Elf Boy went to the river.' The above sentences mean that the principle of justice is created for the first time and that in order for this to work energy must descend the vertical continuum and interact with the horizontal continuum of the grid, the central axis by which insight brings forth cultural evolution.

'He found Fish Maiden relaxing by the water' means that from now on there will be a tendency to forget to live from a place of harmonious balance, and that justice is created at this point in the archetypal world of God's creation of the cosmos because the scales of balance are a necessary and constant part of the process, ' "Good morning, Fish Maiden," he said 'means that perceptual reality is created at this point, to be known later as the House of the Shattering Light, meaning that life is in continual flux and change. 'Elf Boy went over to where Fish Maiden was drying and her mouth was beginning to open' means that greatness through conscious dialogue is necessary in search of insight. ' "I must return to the water as I have been out too long' means that greatness would be the way to compare one's achievements to greatness. 'Elf Boy said, "Could you wait a while longer?" ' indicates the spontaneity of life. 'Fish Maiden replied, "I cannot stay out of the water for very long' means that unity is created. 'Which made Elf Boy angry' means that life is always in a state of interaction of heat created by effort, necessary for higher evolution, and that what is important here is that work is worship. And we are also presented with the idea of intentional suffering, and that is the way in which we move into trusting life, and that this is what connects us to inner as well as to the cosmic truth of awareness.

'On his way back he picked five cones from a tall spruce tree, and took them to where Magpietail Boy was stuck on the cliff' means that standing at the base foundation of the horizontal place we can move for the first time down the vertical continuum for greater insight. 'Elf Boy said, "I will help you to get out of here, if you will catch but one of these five spruce cones' means that the story teller is saying that in order to stay open to revelations from above we must be able to catch them, as with new ideas that come into our Awakened Awareness. Here too we are interested in the five steps that can lead us to higher awareness, which are the five vowel sounds of vibration.

'I am going to drop one at a time and if you miss them, you will not be able to get out', means that until we understand the inner meaning of revelation, higher greatness cannot be achieved. ' "Very well, I will try to catch them." Then Elf Boy dropped one of them, but Magpietail Boy missed it. He dropped him another one, but still Magpietail Boy did not catch it. Now Elf Boy scared him by saying, "You must catch this one because it is the last." "Yes, I will catch it," said Magpietail Boy, but he missed it as well.' "Well then, I suppose you will just have to stay up there as that is all I had," Elf Boy said. Magpietail Boy said nothing, but Elf Boy could see that he was beginning to look very frightened' introduces the concept of separation dividing wholeness in half, and we have the meaning of fear in the story. 'Then Elf Boy took out another spruce cone. "Now, this time I am telling you it is the last one, and if you do not catch it, I cannot help you get out of here" ' means we will be ready for insights when they appear. 'As Elf Boy spoke he dropped the cone, and Magpietail Boy reached out and caught it. "All right," Elf Boy said. "Drop the cone and let it fall straight down" ' means that the true path in life is the straight path up the vertical continuum for higher and higher levels of insight. 'He followed these instructions, and when the cone hit the ground a spruce tree grew up beside him next to the cliff' means the feminine and the masculine are created for the first time. The passive, which is the feminine, descends until it touches matter and the active, which is the masculine, is created at that point. The metaphor of the pine cones expresses this idea. 'Now, you can climb down the spruce tree' means that now physical life has a way of expression; in metaphor the spruce tree means greatness connected to the self, and the way to climb greatness is through the use of the passive–active principles. With a sigh of relief Magpietail Boy did so' means that in fact now life sighs with relief because the potential transformative possibilities can occur. ' "Thank you for your help," he said, and then he told Elf Boy the whole story of what had happened to him. "Very well," said Elf Boy, leading him over to a fallen tree. Elf Boy picked out a woodworm and gave it to Magpietail Boy, and told him, "You must place this worm by Yellow Corn Woman's bed" ' means that in order to be open to conscious awareness we must not be afraid to begin the journey to higher insights. "When you get home, do not tell her what you are doing, and you must not quarrel with her." Elf Boy then went home.'

'When Magpietail Boy got home, he sat awhile. Yellow Corn Woman gave him something to eat, and then they both went to bed. Magpietail Boy put the worm next to where Yellow Corn Woman slept and it entered her navel that night while she was asleep. The worm ate up all her entrails and Yellow Corn Woman died. And so Magpietail Boy lived happily ever after, alone' means that higher conscious awareness has been achieved. It also introduces the idea of looking at life as a chain, made out of connected moments, with each link an opportunity to start anew, and that is really life beginning-ness with no ending-ness to it.

And now you have a tale.

I have included two more Picuris children's stories for your enjoyment, only this time without any of the translations of their meaning, so enjoy them just as they appear — or you may want to look for the inner meanings yourselves. Enjoy!

12   Sengerepove'ena Fights with the Sun

Long, long, long ago the people were living at San Juan Pueblo. And Sengerepove'ena, the great hunter, lived there with his wife and two children. Every day he went out hunting for deer, for that was the only way that he could feed his children.

One day he went out and walked all day but could not see the tracks of a deer. As he sat down to rest on a log, he wondered, 'Why do I not find any deer today?' He picked up his bow, saying', 'If only a four-horned deer would come out I could shoot him at once.' And then right before him stood a four-horned deer. He drew his bow to aim but the Deer spoke to him. 'Do not shoot me, my friend,' it said. Frightened Sengerepove'ena sat still. The Deer went over to where he was sitting. 'My friend, will you listen to me? Within five days you must make five quivers and arrows to fill them. When you finish these you must be ready, for the Sun that is helping the people to live and giving them light is going to make war on you. In five days' time you must come this way again, with your children, for here you will meet the Sun and you will have to fight with the Sun. That is all that I have to say. Act like a man,' said the Deer. Then Sengerepove'ena got up and started home.

He did not bring any deer. As he entered his village, the people said, 'Sengerepove'ena is not bringing a deer this time.' For every time he had gone hunting he had brought home a deer. He was very sad. 'My husband', said his wife when he reached home, 'why did you not kill a deer today? There must be something the matter with you. As long as you have been going out hunting, you have never come back without a deer.' Sadly he sat down as she placed something to eat in his bowl. He ate two or three mouthfuls and then got up. 'My wife,' he said, 'while I was hunting, as I was about to shoot a deer, the Deer spoke to me and began telling me that five days from today the Sun is going to make war on me. He also said that within five days I must make five quivers and fill them with arrows. In five days' time I must return to the same place I saw the Deer today and there the Sun and I will meet, and we will have a fight. You and our two children must get ready.'

Then Sengerepove'ena did nothing but make arrows during the next five days, and by the night of the fourth day he had five quivers ready, filled with arrows. He said, 'In the morning we shall see who is the braver, who is more of a man, the Sun or I.'

Sengerepove'ena and his wife and his two children arose before daylight the next day and ate breakfast. Then Sengerepove'ena put on his war paint, adorning his face with red and his body with white spots. 'Come let us go, my dear ones, it matters not what happens to me. My wife, should I be injured or killed, take our two children with you to the home of their grandfather and grandmother. There you may live in safety and in peace. There will you be taken care of.' Then they started on their journey to the place where the Deer had spoken. Once there a tall man, in war paint, with an eagle feather at the back of his head and a shining ornament on his forehead, came out from the north-east. The two men began to shoot arrows at each other from a distance, and then they came closer to each other. As they approached they were empty-ing their quivers until each had only one quiver left. Try as they could, they could not hit each other although they were still drawing nearer until each shot his last arrow. Dropping their bows and empty quivers, they began to fight hand-to-hand. As they wrestled Sengerepove'ena was thrown down, and the Sun took out his knife and severed Sengere-pove'ena's neck. As soon as his neck was severed the Sun took Sengere-pove'ena's wife to the heavens where he lived and the children ran away to their grandparents. The Sun took Sengerepove'ena's head with him.

When the two children arrived at their grandparents' home and told their story of what had just happened, their grandfather said, 'Very well, I shall make shinny[4] sticks for you, and when I finish them you must put them on your backs and go to look for your parents. For while you are searching you will need them.' Grandfather finished the shinny sticks and the two children set off to look for their parents.

They had been on the road for three or four days when they came to the home of Old Man Woodrat and Old Woman Woodrat. The Wood-rats said, 'Little children, where are you going?' 'We are going to look for our parents,' the boys replied. 'Very well,' said the Woodrats, and they each took two little sticks from their ears and gave one to each of the boys. 'As you are hunting for your parents, should there be any betting, you could rub these on yourselves.'

The little boys went on their way. Soon they came to the home of the White Butterflies. 'Little boys, where are you going?' the White Butterflies said. 'We are going to look for our parents,' the little boys replied. 'Very well,' said the White Butterflies. 'Take this white paint, for where you are going to look for your parents you may need it.' The little boys took the white paint and went on with their journey.

Next, they came to the home of the Black Butterflies, who said, 'Where are you going, little boys?' 'We are going to look for our parents,' the little boys said to the Black Butterflies. The Black Butterflies said, 'Very well, take this black paint, for where you are going to look for your parents you may need it.' They took the black paint and moved on.

As they went on their way, soon they came to the home of the Yellow Butterflies. The Yellow Butterflies asked 'Little boys, where are you going?' The little boys replied 'We are going to look for our parents.' 'Very well,' said the Yellow Butterflies, 'if you take this yellow paint, where you are going to look for your parents you may need it.' The little boys took the yellow paint and went on their way.

They soon came to the home of the Blue Butterflies, who said 'Where are you going, little boys?' 'We are going to look for our parents,' said the little boys. The Blue Butterflies said, 'Very well, take this blue paint, for where you are going to look for your parents you may need it.' The little boys took the blue paint and went on their way.

As they continued their journey, they came upon a Special Creature, with wings, that resembled a crow. 'Where are you going, little boys?' said the Special Creature. 'We are going to look for our parents,' said the little boys. 'Very well,' said the Special Creature, 'have you any white, black and yellow paint?' The little boys said 'We have.' 'Good. If you can paint my feathers as I tell you I will take you up to where the Sun lives,' said the Special Creature with wings. 'Good', exclaimed the little boys, 'we will paint your feathers as you wish.' 'Very well,' said the Special Creature with wings, 'paint my head white and my bill and legs yellow, and here on my breast paint white, and paint my tail white with black at the tip. After you have painted me in this way I can then fly you to where the Sun lives.' 'Very well,' the two boys said, 'we will paint you as you wish'. So they painted the Special Creature, and when they had finished they called him the Eagle, which is why the Eagle looks as he does today. 'Very well,' said the Eagle, 'now sit on my back and hold tight, for I am about to fly. As soon as I take off close your eyes tightly for you must not look until I tell you to.' 'Very well,' said the two boys as they climbed upon the Eagle's back.

The Eagle began to fly, he climbed higher and higher as he circled, and then he landed. 'Now, open your eyes,' said the Eagle.

As they did so they beheld a strange-looking land. 'Here, little boys, is the Sun's land. Your mother is staying over there in that white house. The Sun has taken her for his wife, and your father's head is at the house of the Morning Star. Every morning he plays shinny with your father's head. So early tomorrow you must go to where he plays shinny. He will make fierce noises, but do not fear him. Should he ask you any questions, do not be afraid to answer him; should he invite you to play shinny, you must be willing to play with him, but you must not hit your father's head. Try only to hit the Morning Star's shinny sticks. He will have about ten, and you must try to break them all. When you break the last one the Morning Star will drop dead and then you must take your father's head and come back here again. I will be waiting.'

The little children did as the Eagle had said. Early the next morning they heard fierce noises. 'The Morning Star is playing shinny with our father's head,' they said 'let us go and meet him. We will do as the Eagle has told us to do, and we will win.' They went to where the Morning Star was making noises, and he said to them, 'Why do you come here, little boys? No creature is brave enough to come to where I am; why, not even a little bird will come here. Now I shall eat both of you up.' 'We are here, anyway,' the little boys said bravely. 'Very well,' said the Morning Star, 'here is your father's head, and every morning I play shinny with it. If you are here looking for your parents, let us play shinny with your father's head and whoever wins shall keep it.'

They began to play and the little children, instead of hitting the shinny ball, hit the Morning Star's shinny sticks. They hit one stick after another, breaking them as they did so and when the last stick was broken the Morning Star dropped dead. 'We have won our father's head,' said the little children. 'Now let us return to the Eagle.' So they took the head and ran to where the Eagle was waiting for them.

'How did you make out, little boys?' said the Eagle. 'Well,' said the two boys, 'we have won our father's head.' 'Very well,' said the Eagle, 'now you may go and fetch your mother. When you return with her I will take all of you down to the earth again. You must go to where she is staying when it gets dark, for only then will the Sun be asleep. You must spit the earsticks that the Woodrats gave you on to him while he is asleep, and he will not be able to awaken. Then you must bring your mother here.' 'All right,' said the little boys.

So as soon as night fell, they left to go and fetch their mother. When they entered the room of the house they found the Sun asleep. They spat the earsticks of the Woodrats on him, and soon the Sun was in a very deep sleep. They took their mother and carried her to where the Eagel awaited.

'How did you make out?' said the Eagle. 'Well,' said the little boys. 'Very well,' said the Eagle, 'now the three of you sit on my back, close your eyes tightly as soon as I take off, and do not open them until I have landed upon the Earth.' Then they got onto his back, and flew off, circled down and landed on the ground. 'Now,' said the Eagle, 'take your father's head to a dark place and do not look at it for five days. After that time your father will return to the flesh again.'

When the little children and their mother reached home they did as the Eagle had told them. After five days they went to look, and they found Sengerepove'ena as he had been before. They all lived happily ever afterwards.

And now you have a tale.

13   The Old Giantess and the Brother and Sister Fawns

LONG, LONG, LONG AGO THERE LIVED an Old Giantess at Wetholapawa'an. She went hunting every day and killed whatever she could – rabbits, chipmunks, tree squirrels, and so on – and brought them home.

On one particularly fine day she threw her shawl over her shoulders, took up her walking stick, and started off for Pin'oma. On her way she came upon a brother and a sister Fawn fast asleep. Slowly and quietly she crept towards them, glancing to her left and then to her right as she did so. She quickly threw her shawl over the young Fawns and caught them up. 'Hooray!' the Old Giantess exclaimed, 'I now have two little Fawns. I shall take them home and feed them well to fatten them up, and then I will roast them and eat them all up!' She gathered up her shawl with the little Fawns in it, put it on her back and carried them home.

The Old Giantess turned the little Fawns loose inside the house so they could walk about. Every day she fed them corn mush and whatever else she could find. Slowly the young Fawns began to grow, and as they grew up, they became accustomed to the Old Giantess and her house. She used to take them outside to play every day. The little Fawns would walk up the road for a distance and then would return home again.

The Old Giantess kept feeding them very well, and they began to grow larger and larger. Every day the Old Giantess would say, 'Little ones, I can feel that your little kidneys are getting nice and fat.' The little Fawns said to each other, 'The Old Giantess feels our little kidneys every day and is likely to roast us and eat us all up! We must run away!' Every day they became more and more afraid. One night they agreed, 'Tomorrow we must run away before the Old Giantess roasts us and eats us all up.'

The next morning the Old Giantess gave them their breakfast and took them outside to play. 'Now is the time for us to run away,' they said. 'We will go up the road as usual, but this time we will keep going and will not return to be roasted and eaten up by the Old Giantess.' And so they started off. The Old Spider Woman, who lived nearby, was sitting on the roof of her house enjoying the view. As she watched the little Fawns going along the road, she said aloud, 'The little Fawns are running away from the Old Giantess.' When the Old Giantess heard this, she thought to herself, 'They can only go as far as the top of the hill and then they will come back home.' The little Fawns were already quite a distance up the road. The Old Giantess heard the Old Spider Woman say again and again from the top of her house, 'The little Fawns of the Old Giantess are running away.' 'Can this be so?' wondered the Old Giantess to herself. She put her shawl over her shoulders, took her walking stick and went outside. She looked up the road and saw that her little Fawns were already quite far away. 'Sure enough, my little Fawns are running away from me,' she said in disbelief, 'I must hurry after them and bring them back home.'

The little Fawns went along swiftly and soon came to Paxepeta on the river. As they passed through the settlement they came to where Big Nostril lay on his blanket looking for lice. 'What is the matter, little Fawns? Where are you going?' Big Nostril said to them. 'We are running away because the Old Giantess feels our kidneys every day, and we fear she will eat us all up. Will you please hide us?' 'Very well,' said Big Nostrils, 'step into my nostrils.' The little Fawns did as they were told. Shortly the Old Giantess came along, huffing and puffing and all sweaty from hurrying. 'Big Nostril, my little Fawns have run away from me. Have you seen them?' said the Old Giantess. 'No fawns have come by today. I am doing nothing but lying here on my blanket looking for lice,' and having said that he threw his head back and let out a very big sneeze. The little Fawns flew out of his nose and sailed far away. 'For goodness' sake, Big Nostril, my Fawns are way over yonder.' The Old Giantess clutched her shawl around her and followed behind them, huffing and puffing as she went.

The little Fawns went along quickly, and soon they came to where Old Ploughmaker was making a plough. As he examined it on both sides to see if it was true, he said, 'What is the matter, little Fawns? Where are you going?' 'We are running away from the Old Giantess for we fear she will roast us and eat us all up, because she feels our little kidneys every day. So please hide us, if you will,' said the little Fawns. 'Very well, both of you step into the crack in the plough.' So they did as they were told. Shortly the Old Giantess came along, huffing and puffing and all sweaty from hurrying, with her shawl round her shoulders and her walking stick in hand. She stopped where the Old Ploughmaker was working. 'Ploughmaker, have you seen my little Fawns anywhere near here?' said the Old Giantess. 'I have been busy making my ploughs, and have not seen any little Fawns,' he said, as he checked to see if the plough was true. The sound of his hammer could be heard for quite a distance, and suddenly he hit his plough a good, hard blow, and the little Fawns went flying out. 'Oh Ploughmaker, my Fawns are way over yonder,' she said. The little Fawns had gone quite a distance along the road. The Old Giantess hurried along, following behind the Fawns, again trying to catch up with them.

The Fawns followed the river to the dam where Old Man Beaver was basking in the sunshine by the water's edge. 'What is the matter, little Fawns? Where are you going?' said the Old Man Beaver. 'We are running away because the Old Giantess will roast us and eat us all up because she feels our little kidneys every day. Can you please carry us across the river to the other side?' said the little Fawns. 'Very well,' said the Old Man Beaver, 'climb upon my back and I will swim across the river with you.' The little Fawns did as they were told, and he carried them across the river. When they got to the other side Old Man Beaver said, 'You must go to Kuhane'ai where the Snakes live. They will tell you where to go.' So the little Fawns went along their way to Kuhane'ai.

Shortly afterwards the Old Giantess came along, huffing and puffing and all sweaty from hurrying, with her shawl round her shoulders and her walking stick in hand, to where Old Man Beaver was sunning himself by the river. 'Old Man Beaver, have you seen my little Fawns?' 'Yes, I have, and I just carried them across the river. They are just over yonder.' 'Well then, carry me across, so that I can catch them before they get away from me again,' said the Old Giantess as she gathered up her shawl and walking stick. 'Climb upon my back,' said the Old Man Beaver. She did so, and he started swimming across the river. But as he reached the middle of the river, where the water was deepest, he suddenly turned himself over and the Old Giantess was thrown in. She struggled as she sank under the water and came up again. But finally she reached the shore and crawled out of the water and said, 'For goodness' sake! How bothersome it is to have all these interruptions when all I am trying to do is make a living. My little Fawns are getting further and further away from me.' She shook herself dry and again began to follow the little Fawns.

The little Fawns did as they were told and went on their way to Kuhane'ai where the Snakes lived. They approached the estufa carefully, and the Snakes heard someone outside. One of them was sent to look around, and he reported, 'There are two little Fawns standing outside.' The leader said to him, 'Let them come in then. Go and invite them to join us.' The Snake went out and invited the little Fawns to join them in their estufa. 'Come in, little ones,' said the Snake leader as they entered, and found that the whole estufa was full of snakes.

'Here, sit down, little Fawns. Be comfortable. Tell me, what have you come for?' The little Fawns sat down and told the Snakes, 'The Old Giantess felt our little kidneys every day and wants to roast us and eat us all up, and so we decided to run away. When we got to the river, Old Man Beaver carried us across on his back and told us to come see you. That is why we are here.' 'Very well,' said the Snake leader. And no sooner had he spoken than the Old Giantess was heard, huffing and puffing, outside the estufa. As she arrived, all sweating, at the roof door, she called out, 'Insider, are my little Fawns in there?' 'Yes, they are in here. Please come in and get them,' invited the Snake leader, 'No, bring them out to me,' said the Old Giantess fearfully. 'Come in and get them,' replied the Snake leader. She hesitated and then started to climb down the ladder. She only had one more step to take before reaching the floor when she heard the rattle of a Snake that was lying beneath the ladder. 'Oh, oh,' cried the Old Giantess as she scrambled back up the ladder and out of the estufa. When she finally got outside, she started running home, and so great was her fear of snakes that she was frightened by all the sticks lying along the road on her way.

The leader of the Snakes said to the little Fawns, 'Now, little Fawns, you can go to the mountains where you belong, and once there you must mate and increase your number. When you, little boy, reach Pin'o'ai you must go towards Jicarita Mountain, and there you must mate and bring forth. And you, little girl, must go north-east from there and mate and bring forth there among the mountains.' And so the leader of the Snakes bid them farewell. As they went on their way they said to each other, 'Now we are going to be together for a short while but we will be lonesome as we separate and go alone in the mountains. But we must do as we were told.'

When they came to Pin'o'ai they tearfully bade farewell to each other, and then parted. The little boy Fawn went towards Jicarita Mountain, and the little girl Fawn went to the north-east. As the little boy Fawn went on alone he grew tired and sighed in his loneliness, 'I wonder how my poor little sister Fawn is getting along. The Snakes did not send us together; they sent us on separate paths.' The little girl Fawn cried as she went along her pathway, 'Oh me, oh my,' she said, 'I wonder how my

older brother is getting along. The Snakes did not send us together;
they sent us on separate paths.'

When they arrived at their destinations, they did as they had been
told and mated and brought forth many of their kind, and this is the
reason the deer live there among the mountains and are plentiful.

And now you have a tale.

PART THREE

14 The Six Passions

HERE I ATTEMPT TO SHOW HOW the six passions — jealousy, anger, greed, pride, attachment and mental obscuration — can be positive impulses that, when used purposefully, can lead us to greater insightful living.

JEALOUSY

Jealousy is connected to the possession of someone or something physical. One of the steps to changing jealousy is to redirect it away from the physical level towards one of seeking insights in our lives.

ANGER

When we are experiencing anger, we are stuck between Believing We Exist and Awakened Awareness. Our inner sense of Awakened Awareness wants to move beyond anger while the Believing We Exist wants to fight or flee as a way to solve the conflict between the two. And unless the process moves to the next step of reconciliation the anger will continue. Anger is a positive impulse because it seeks to find a solution to the conflict, and when this happens new insights come.

The state of conflict is when insight happens. Insights come forth into bridging Believing We Exist and Awakened Awareness. In the moment of insight the physical body sighs a breath of relief, and this is the way of recognizing that a shift has occurred.

If the anger becomes destructive (and it usually does), it will move towards the destruction of the person, place or thing, because it wants to open up the space in order to bring forth new insight.

Greed

Greed is a heightened desire to accumulate possessions. It is embedded very deeply in the psyche and identifies with the Existence of Existence. Again to re-establish greed is to redirect the intense desire towards seeking new insight.

Pride

Pride may be derived from the delight of satisfaction in one's achievements, possessions, children, for instance. However, after a while, we begin to associate our pride with them, and consequently we get stuck at that level. To change the pride level we need to move to a more open place, where we become receptive to new insights and establish our pride around the delight of achievement on insight. The end result of this type of shift will yield us more and more insights which will increase our possessions, and lead us to a freer, more open relationship with our children.

Attachments

What we experience with the physical body we automatically own. Why? Because our eyes perceive what we see and establish it as our own private territorial space. We own it.

In the first step towards releasing ourselves from attachments we try to obscure them mentally, thereby removing ourselves from the risk of attachment. However, we will soon find that research is necessary if we seek to sense and investigate the attachment.

The second step is to see how and why the attachment occurred in the first place. Once that has been ascertained we find that we are attached to a person, place or thing because we identify it with our Believing We Exist, because the identification with it gives us placement. Our attachments help us to define the belief that we are 'alive' and existing, and therefore it is difficult to release or let go of any attachments.

When we have attachment, and want to continue with it, we are really plugging the gap of our 'inner spark plug'. We fill that gap with our attachment, therefore preventing the spark of insight from firing the light of Awakened Awareness.

MENTAL OBSCURATION

In mental obscuration we are ignoring our ability to see the truth in a given situation. We do this by taking away the purpose of the experience, and as we do so our relationship to the unity in diversity in all of life disappears too. Consequently we separate ourselves consciously from cosmic truth.

15   List of Insights

Insight 1: I want to share in 'Crossing the River', listening with my ears and seeing with my eyes so that my whole body was listening, because 60 per cent of what I was hearing was being received by my physical body, and 40 per cent was being received by my eyes.   10

Insight 2: Whatever we see or experience outside our physical body (or what I call our 'outer landscape') teaches our inner landscape, thereby imparting meaning by way of the physical body.   15

Insight 3: When the physical heart is pumping the physical blood of the body it is affirming the act; the blood is receptivity and the action of the physical body is reconciliation.   18

Insight 4: Hearing with my physical ears connected me directly to physical activity; I understood that work was another way of worshipping, that listening and working were one and the same thing.   23

Insight 5: It is through culture that evolution occurs. The Tiwas believe that only through meritorious work and/or high ethical behaviour can one human being be awarded not only the highest potential but the opportunity of carrying the whole tribal essence in and of itself in the individual. And that once this responsibility is bestowed it is to be carried on the basis of continual vigilance, so that only the highest ethical behaviour be maintained.   26

Insight 6: When a vision or idea is received the recipient also is

given the power to carry it through because that is the nature of
insight.   29

Insight 7: An ancient event or an event in the distant future can be
experienced through metaphor in the present.   31

Insight 8: That one will experience in many instances through
ceremonies a moment of clairvoyance: one will see that which one
may be seeking at some future time, prior to the moment of
encountering it in a physical experience.   37

Insight 9: As human beings we have an innate sense of knowing
that says that everything we see we automatically own or possess,
therefore we are, by pre-conditioning, territorial.   38

Insight 10: I knew that he was making reference to Picuris mountain
and that he had been sent by the voice that had spoken to me that
day while I was standing next to the deer on Wooden Cross
mountain.   40

Insight 11: Shattering light was in those moments when we are
between slices of light, or reading between the gaps that give us
insight.   42

Insight 12: Time washing was the metaphor and the physical
experience was the bonding with it. Also it reminded me of when I
used to watch the spirit of someone who has just died cross over
and go through the tunnel from the physical world to the spiritual. 42

Insight 13: The deer means to name knowingness; puma, to have
visionary capacities; rabbit, to be higher states of healing; coyote,
to move upwards and onwards along the cosmic grid; and squirrels, to evolve beyond self-imposed limitations.   43

Insight 14: I understood that there are six passions capable of
keeping us from our insightful capacities if we allow them to rule
us. They are attachment, jealousy, pride, greed, anger and mental
obscuration. However, I found that if I could use these passions
creatively I could go beyond them to my true nature of staying
wide awake and receptive to new insights.   43

Insight 15: We scale the walls of our own unclarities, and in so doing give direction to the evolutionary progress of culture, to the advancement of human life on the Earth. 44

Insight 16: I had just experienced some of the metaphors in the story. 45

Insight 17: As I walked home down the canyon trail I realized that I could only absorb the teachings I had received at the waterfall through physical actions, drink them into my soul and then fully integrate them by walking and talking about my experiences. 45

Insight 18: There must be only one true reality and that it is all taking place within the reality of *The One Great Mystery* called 'Light of Living Truth.' 47

Insight 19: To sweat is to transcend duality. The earth was the self as the ever-unfolding flower and we, her children, were evolving with her. 49

Insight 20: In my physical body each light was a biological cell and there were so many of them. 50

Insight 21: Seven meant for me 'a new path', and that if I wanted to have new insights, I could build a fire every seventh of the month to ensure continuity of insight. 51

Insight 22: Apparently, by living and staying focused in the medium of our talents, our innate intelligence through metaphor alongside experience keeps our physical body connected to enlightenment. 52

Insight 23: At the time of writing the child that was given to the Earth in metaphor is nine years old. 53

16   Learning how to Think through the Use of the Five Vowel Sounds

TRAINING OUR MINDS ON HOW TO think was as important in ancient times as it is today. The world always needs good, clear thinkers so that the human culture can advance.

The evolutionary process of our beautiful planet relies on us to bring forth clarity to the world. It is vital in today's world since nature created our physical bodies to be instruments, capable of listening for insights. We now have the opportunity to bring forth that new insight to the world. Therefore I am suggesting in this chapter that by chanting the vowel sounds out loud we can train our minds to evoke new insights in our lives. A, E, I, O and U, when chanted in this order, helps to train the mind to seek these insights.

There are five vowels therefore five steps to the process in this practice.

Practice

Take five deep, slow breaths to clear the mind and body before starting. Once you have cleansed yourself of all thoughts, begin the practice.

Step 1   Imagine that you are looking, sensing or feeling your whole body, and then chant out loud the vowel A, sounded as 'aah'. Do this practice for one minute while timing yourself.

Step 2   Cover your right eye with your right hand and focus your left eye on an object in front of you, studying it in detail, while chanting out loud the vowel E, sounded as 'eh', for one minute.

Now while repeating the E sound remove your right hand place your left hand on your left eye and focus on the same object in front of you for one minute.

Did you notice that when the right eye was focused on the object in front of you it experienced a different image from that of the left eye? In Step 1 you were training your mind to see the whole object as a single unit. For instance, unity in diversity. In Step 2 you were training your mind to recognize the polarities, as in male/female, or opposites, as in hot/cold. Go back and open and close your right and left eyes rapidly, and notice that they are receiving different images of the same object. Do this until you feel you have integrated this step.

By chanting the vowel E 'eh' sound you probably had the insight that you were connecting the right and left hemisphere, that is the right and left brain, to your physical body through the use of sound vibration. This simple practice, performed over the period of twenty years, helped me to think with my whole body, to see, feel and sense existing conditions in my life.

Step 3   Now chant the vowel I, sounded as 'eee' while both your eyes are open and focused on the same object in front of you. Do this for one minute.

This practice is important because it trains the brain and the body to reconcile differences in polarities or opposites.

Step 4   Now chant the vowel O, sounded as 'ohh', while looking at the object in front of you. Ask yourself what is the purpose of the object.

This practice is important because it trains the brain/body to look for and to seek the purpose or direction of physical activity toward a given goal.

Step 5   Now chant the vowel U, sounded as 'ooo', for one minute, while asking yourself what are the other potential possibilities that the object in front of you can be used for, other than its ordinary accepted standard use. For instance, let's just say that the object is a pencil. Think of at least three other ways to use it other than as a writing instrument. Be creative!

In summary, the vowel sounds train the body/mind how to think as follows:

1. A—'aah' sees unity in diversity.
2. E—'eh' recognizes polarities and opposites.
3. I—'eee' sees reconciliation of polarities or of opposites.
4. O—'ohh' sees the purposes of physical action to be taken toward a particular direction.
5. U—'ooo' sees the potential possibilities in a given direction that is taken.
6. Combine the five vowels in the same order, A, E, I, O and U, and create a singing chant while dancing the five-step process for about five minutes.

Why, Because by singing them you keep your body and brain open to new insights, and the action of dancing expands awakened awareness.

Finally, the last and perhaps the most important step in the process is to use the new insights that you receive in a purposeful way in your life.

The following paragraph gives a further explanation of what is happening in the body when we use sound. The vowel sound waves, when we chant them, connect all the different parts of our physical bodies to the right and left hemispheres of our brains. Why? Because within the loud sound there seems to be a silent sound, resonating off the audible sound, that embodies the vibration level of the letter that is being chanted. This is important if a connection is to be made between the brain and the body. As we chant we shift from the material experiencing of the body to that of the brain waves.

Here is one example of how chanting worked for me in 1984 in Bernalillo, New Mexico. After doing an absent healing on a person five hundred miles away in Texas, I went to bed. I entered into a deep sleep around 2am, when all of a sudden I felt a surge of energy come right through the top of my body and the bottoms of my feet. I woke up with a jolt, because the force was so strong that it bounced me up, but not off, the mattress. I looked up and there was a hole in the roof of my bedroom, and up in the sky I could see a choir of angelic beings, standing on clouds, holding books in their hands. They were looking towards me and singing the most beautiful music I have ever heard. At that moment I knew I was experiencing in metaphor the healing of the man I had been sending healing energy to. Early the next morning his mother called and said 'Last night was the first night my son has slept real well.'

There have been other experiences in the last twenty years in which I have seen healings in metaphors, and I believe the practices that I have outlined contributed directly to my visionary experiences.

Training the mind to bring new insights into our daily life is the key to existing purposefully.

Next I would like to share with you an understanding that the nature of insight is such that it is the interaction between opposing temperatures, as in hot and cold thought patterns; as they collide they create new insight.

17 How and Why Insight Occurs

Step 1   Imagine that conscious thought is moving. This can be symbolically represented by a line followed by a space. The line symbolizes everything that the brain knows in that moment.

Illustration No. 1

Brain   ────── ────── ────── ────── ────── ──────

Step 2   Imagine next that a second line, which is solid, runs parallel to the first line, as in the example that follows.

Illustration No. 2

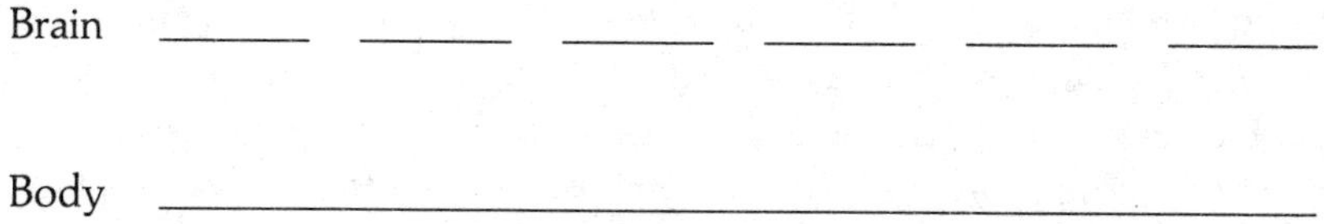

Brain   ────── ────── ────── ────── ────── ──────

Body   ──

This second solid line represents the physical body which is constantly returning messages to the brain as impulses and which it sends via its neuromuscular connections, as in the next example.

Illustration No. 3

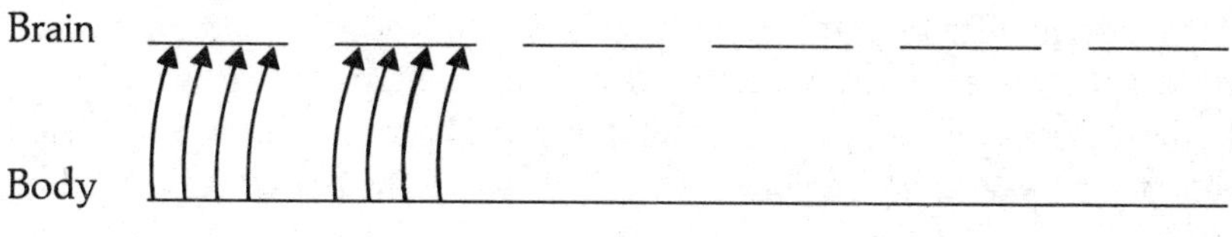

Brain   ⤴⤴⤴⤴ ⤴⤴⤴⤴ ────── ────── ────── ──────

Body   │││││ │││││ ────────────────────────────

In this example, the brain is acting out what the body is receiving from its surrounding environment.

Step 3   Now imagine that the salt, sugar and water content of the physical body is lowered through fasting for a given period of time (2 to 3 days), and that the body is involved in some physical exertion. The physical body will begin to increase the number of impulses it sends to the brain, as in the next example.

These impulses tell the brain that it is time to feed both brain and body. However, if the person is consciously working towards receiving insight, and continues, for example, exercising the physical body, at this point the physical body will increase the impulses it is sending to the brain, as shown here.

Illustration No. 4

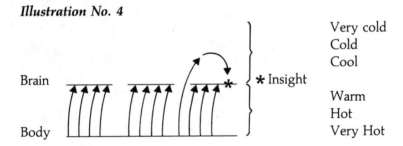

Because of the higher impulse rate, one of them can miss the conscious thought pattern (represented here by the broken line), and travel higher, from the hot levels of form to the cold levels of pure Truth. The magnetic quality of the brain then attracts the impulse back down again. At the point when the impulse touches the brain again, an insight is released. In this way, new insights or visionary experiences take place and are instantly incorporated into the conscious brainwave patterns. In the next instant the brain will send the insight back down to the body for later reference, and a heightened state of awareness will prevail throughout the physical body in that moment.

The question to ask is what actually happens after the impulse travels higher and beyond the conscious thought pattern. I believe the answer is that as the impulse wave travels further and further away from its origin, symbolically speaking it begins to cool down. At the point of impact and re-entry into the conscious thought pattern, the person's body will feel full of light, or enlightenment, because the two opposite forces of cold and hot, when they collide, shock the pattern of the body and the brain to a new and higher level. A sense of reconciliation then permeates throughout the physical body.

Why? Because when the two opposites touch they create a momentary explosion in which a new higher conscious thought pattern is created. The physical body wave pattern moves up to where the former conscious thought pattern was originally seated, as in the following example, and the original level of conscious thought is correspondingly one level higher also.

Illustration No. 5
New conscious thought pattern
at the higher level

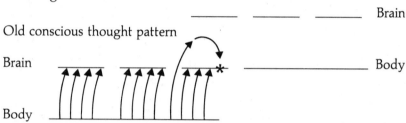

The bottom line disappears altogether because the level of the body's conscious awareness has shifted to a higher level creating re-orientation. Hence the two opposite forces of hot and cold have reached a point of reconciling their differences.

In summary, it is the hot and cold of the impulses that bring forth insights at the moment of impact. It is the collision that creates the insights, because in the reconciliation process they move to a much higher level; similarly, in human relationships, after reconciliation a higher level is achieved. There is also a very old idea that the physical reality of the cosmos was created by the process just described but at a cosmic level — a cosmic leap which resulted in our present physical reality.

In Summary

In the Introduction I explained that Tiwa is a metaphoric language, and that comparing it with the English language began to teach me about the relationships between metaphor, and how one might connect it to everyday experience. For example, 'Go bring the dog' when spoken in Tiwa (*qui kohl me*) translated to: *qui* – watchfulness; *kohl* – to bring to; *me* – to go get; hence to go get and bring to (me) watchfulness. Therefore when the two forms are put together they translate so:

Experience – English – Go bring the dog.
Metaphor – Tiwa – To go get and bring to (me) watchfulness.

So when one can see through the eyes of the poet one can find the insights in daily experiences that can lead to new meaning. Another example I attempt to make in the Introduction is when I cast metaphor as 'Awareness that is Awake' and the physical experience as 'Believing We Exist'. So that the actual experience of going to get the dog is a physical one in ordinary reality, and that of the metaphor is that of the metaphoric (poetic) explanation of it. Finally, when one can train the mind to jump from any experience to metaphor, one can have purposeful insights that are pertinent to one's personal or universal goals. Consequently one lives each moment with only one objective in mind, and that is to be on the lookout for new insight coming out of daily experiences.

In 'Reading between the Gaps' I discuss how the mind has followed a definite process by which it draws certain conclusions about what is being experienced. I also talk about how early childhood socialization, through the use of children's stories (which are made up of metaphors primarily) can determine how we learn to view our natural physical experiences in adult life.

And finally, I look at the way in which the children's stories and the metaphors they contain begin to teach us how to see our physical experiences as metaphors. As soon as we are sufficiently psychologically mature to think in abstract terms we can put metaphor alongside experience, therefore bridging the gaps between experience and metaphor into insight. I use the myth of Magpietail Boy in my attempts to show this basic phenomenon of 'reading between the gaps'.

In 'Sandy, the Runaway Horse', I explore with the reader only briefly how the physical action of the body under certain heightened states of impending danger can produce heightened telepathic or high psychic capacities. Therefore the experience is connected to metaphor through an intense physical action.

In 'My Grandfather', I attempt to explain a number of qualities that characterize the experiences to metaphor. For instance the physical neck, in metaphor, is the dividing line between the brain and the heart, the head and the body and that which the body eats. It enables the brain and the body to function as one unit, and by maintaining the upper (brain) and the lower (body) connection, the impulses can travel between these two physical areas, so that insight may continue unhampered. In the example that my grandfather gives in the metaphor that we are walking stories, he is showing how the brain processes information that is coming from the body, and vice versa, and how it can be likened to the actual physical walking of the physical body.

In the example 'the people who are most against you are the ones that need you the most' he is showing how the impulse of reconciliation is an integral part of how to move on from stalemate to an active, more productive, natural step in the process of exploring life. When one reconciles stalemate one is then open for insight. And that the real gift in life is going through self-created walls, built of our own uncertainties, and that the unexpected is the insight that appears as a surprise.

In 'The Mountain Race', my physical body becomes consciously associated as the Earth and Sky. In Tiwa thought the Earth is the metaphor for the personal individual or universal self.

'In the Springtime' the skin or surface of the Earth as we live metaphor alongside experience is how we evolve to a new understanding that our experiences of seeking for inner meaning on the Earth allow us to have new insights that lead us to the next stage. That is the transformational potential that comes out of experience. In Tiwa thought 'running at dawn' is the metaphor for the initiating of the day. The dogs are watchfulness, and the cats the curiosity towards the desire to see the truth. The idea of war enters here too and in metaphor means that when there is conflict, reconciliation, followed by the direction of activity leading towards transformational possibilities, is the key to insightful living.

In 'Appearing and Disappearing', the metaphor 'finding without being seen first' tells us to look for insights before they occur. When we pull ourselves consciously out of the moment and disappear out of a situation, we can catch the insight. Why? Because in perceptual reality we are the observer, as well as that which is being observed. In concept that which is not there cannot send feedback to the observer. In the example of the animal tracks, the tracks are philosophically the path of a given direction beyond which lie the potential possibilities for new meaning. For instance, the deer in the story is the principle of knowing-ness, and so I was following the tracks of knowingness. Again it is important to find the metaphor in the experience for new insights to be achieved. In the words 'my early childhood teaching of being seen rather than being heard' interestingly enough means that when parenting teaches the child in this way, he or she learns to listen to the silence *between* the words, where insight is hiding and waiting. Imagine that you are a child, sitting at the breakfast table, listening to two adults talking. Think what it might be like to listen to the spread between the words. Try it sometime; it is fascinating. For instance, 'I am going to work the fields today' is constructed in the Tiwa language in such a way that it speaks between the spaces of the words. Why? Again, because it is a metaphoric language. The Tiwa meaning is 'the making of the self through listening to the goodness that lifts us all is the house of song I will do today'. To listen is to learn to hear the silence speaking through metaphor the experience of meaning.

In 'The Angel in the Cave' I attempt to share with the reader the experience that the sound of spoken language opens the psychic to visionary capacity, because the sound of words collides with the skin of the body which is basically a giant ear. Here I am talking about the idea that the human anatomy is asleep, but that when hit by sound it translates what it hears into metaphor, and that is then transformed into a visionary experience. For instance, let's say that an idea of what is to come, as in premonition, collides with the human anatomy. The mind will receive the information and will convert its meaning into a visual perception. Why? Because ideas or thoughts have substance, and have forms that are flowing from the future to the present or from the past to the present, and the human mind is constructed to receive them naturally.

In the word 'angel' I introduce the vowels A and E. Why? Because these are the sound vibrations that connect us to the spaces between the other words. In repeating the A and E sounds we can experience, in metaphor, the inner meaning of the message of the vision.

In 'The Pumas', the metaphor 'When you have babies you will have deer meat to eat' translated into Tiwa means that when we eat the deer meat of knowingness we will have insights along the path of experience. To eat the knowingness through our experiences and integrate them into our psyche is to achieve the revelations that we are naturally entitled to in life's natural experiences. The voice of the pumas that spoke to me asking me to leave the deer was a very natural human process. When we learn to think from the place of metaphor, we connect ourselves to the past as well as to the future; and through the window of the present moment we can see, through experience, the reconciliatory impulse that is vital and necessary for the unfolding of meaning.

In 'At the Waterfall', as well as throughout the content of this book, I attempt to weave metaphor with experience so that the reader can enjoy the inner meaning of the metaphoric mind. In this particular story I try to show how the Picuris children's stories which were presented in metaphor could eventually appear in natural visionary experiences in my adult life.

The ability to see with my normal vision for long distances, or to see into natural forms, as when I looked through the mountain or far away into the night sky, are again natural capacities we have when the be-ing within remembers that we are already enlightened. And that we already know and can see everything because knowingness is an integral part of our nature.

In 'The Journey with the Mermen' and my visitation with Oceanus (or in Tiwa thought *Ocia-o-ney*, Birther of Babies) I show that we are in principle made up of the cosmic ocean of cosmic thought. When we live through insight we are basically living out of metaphor the cosmic level of cosmic thought. This is birthing and rebirthing itself constantly through the metaphor of cosmic thought by way of our physical experiences.

Next comes the original story of Magpietail Boy, followed by the same story but with translations of the metaphors. I did this so that the reader could gain further insights into metaphor. I also included the stories 'Sengerepov'ena Fights with the Sun' and 'The Old Giantess and the Brother and Sister Fawns' for the reader's enjoyment and to provide an opportunity to find the metaphoric meanings that lie therein.

The chapter 'The Six Passions' is important because these play a very important role in determining how we can begin to train the mind to see the passions of jealousy, anger, greed, pride, attachments and mental obscuration, which when understood properly can be a positive exploration into consciousness.

I have listed the insights from the stories separately so that they can be read all at once so that greater insights into the content of *Beautiful Painted Arrow* can be achieved by studying them.

In 'Learning how to think through the Use of the Five Vowel Sounds' I talk about how the evolutionary processes of mankind take place through culture. The reader does not have to learn to speak Tiwa in order to teach the mind to think through the use of metaphor. Anyone can begin to find the metaphors in the spoken or written English language.

In 'How and Why Insight Occurs' I attempt to show the process by which the brainwaves (impulses) are connected to the physical body, and vice versa, and how and why insight happens. As the impulse misses the brainwave it cools as it moves away, so that when it collides with the hot brainwaves, it is in that moment the insight or visionary ability takes place.

Finally, this book *Beautiful Painted Arrow* is as much about my visionary abilities as that of metaphor alongside experience. And the time has come now when we must look to natural metaphor in the spoken or written languages of the American Indians, or other peoples who have retained the metaphoric languages. For to hear God's voice speaking to us is to listen through the metaphors of the spiritual guidance; God's insights, that we have for so long ignored, and that now return to awaken us to our next highest achievement as a human race; we must remember that *the calling is now ours*.

Notes

Part One

Chapter 2 — My Grandfather

1. This is the migration of the people moving from the underworld to the upper world in the Pueblo myth of creation. *See* Bertha Dutton and Caroline Olin, *Myths and Legends of the Indians of the South-west*, Bellerophon Books, Santa Barbara, CA 93101, 1978.

Chapter 4 — In the Springtime

2. *See* Dutton, *op. cit.*

Chapter 7 — The Pumas

3. *See* Dutton, *op. cit.*

Part Two

Chapter 3 — Sengerepove'ena Fights with the Sun

4. Shinny sticks are used to play the game of shinny which is a ball game rather like hockey.

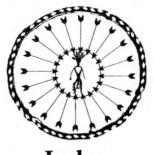

Index